This book is dedicated to my family.

Contents

Swimming

STEPS TO SUCCESS

Scott Bay

HUMAN KINETICS

Library of Congress Cataloging-in-Publication Data

Bay, Scott, 1964- author.

Swimming : steps to success / Scott Bay.
Champaign, IL : Human Kinetics, [2016]
LCCN 2015037240 | ISBN 9781492508441 (print)
  LCSH: Swimming--Training.
LCC GV838.67.T73 B39 2016 | DDC 797.2/1--dc23 LC record available at http://lccn.loc.gov/
2015037240

ISBN: 978-1-4925-0844-1 (print)

The web addresses cited in this text were current as of September 2015, unless otherwise noted.

Acquisitions Editor: Tom Heine
Developmental Editor: Anne Hall
Managing Editor: Elizabeth Evans
Copyeditor: Tom Tiller
Senior Graphic Designer: Keri Evans
Cover Designer: Keith Blomberg
Photograph (cover): miljko/istock.com
Photographs (interior): David Haas
Photo Asset Manager: Laura Fitch
Visual Production Assistant: Joyce Brumfield
Photo Production Manager: Jason Allen
Art Manager: Kelly Hendren
Associate Art Manager: Alan L. Wilborn
Illustrations: © Human Kinetics
Printer: Versa Press

We thank Volusia Flagler YMCA and the city of Daytona Beach as well as Teresa Rand and Joe Woodens for assistance in providing the location for the photo shoot for this book.

Human Kinetics books are available at special discounts for bulk purchase. Special editions or book excerpts can also be created to specification. For details, contact the Special Sales Manager at Human Kinetics.

Printed in the United States of America   10 9 8 7 6 5 4 3 2 1

Human Kinetics
Website: www.HumanKinetics.com

United States: Human Kinetics
P.O. Box 5076
Champaign, IL 61825-5076
800-747-4457
e-mail: info@hkusa.com

Canada: Human Kinetics
475 Devonshire Road Unit 100
Windsor, ON N8Y 2L5
800-465-7301 (in Canada only)
e-mail: info@hkcanada.com

Europe: Human Kinetics
107 Bradford Road
Stanningley
Leeds LS28 6AT, United Kingdom
+44 (0) 113 255 5665
e-mail: hk@hkeurope.com

Australia: Human Kinetics
57A Price Avenue
Lower Mitcham, South Australia 5062
08 8372 0999
e-mail: info@hkaustralia.com

New Zealand: Human Kinetics
P.O. Box 80
Mitcham Shopping Centre, South Australia 5062
0800 222 062
e-mail: info@hknewzealand.com

E6544

Foreword

The world of swimming has been very good to me. Growing up in Winter Haven, Florida, I was able to go from the kid who got cut from other sports to Olympic champion. As a television commentator for swimming, I get to continue my passion for the sport that I love.

I have known Coach Scott Bay for many years, and we've had many great talks about swimming: its history, its evolution, and, most important, the recent advances in technique. We have worked together at several clinics, and we always have a great exchange of ideas and observations. Coach Bay is truly a student of the sport.

In *Swimming: Steps to Success*, Coach Bay explains the elements of technique that are part of good swimming. There will always be variations by elite swimmers, and I encourage you to explore some of your own. This book can serve as a jumping-off point where you can get sound advice on stroke technique and instruction.

So . . . whether you picked up this book out of curiosity or sought it out because you want to see what swimming has to offer, you will enjoy Coach Bay's detailed instruction and continue your journey into the amazing world of fun, fitness, and competition in swimming.

Best wishes to you on your journey!

Rowdy Gaines
Three-time Olympic gold medalist and TV commentator

Climbing the Steps to Swimming Success

Swimming has been practiced as both a sport and a recreational activity for thousands of years. People at the highest levels of competition swim with such grace and ease that it seems almost effortless. For a beginner or novice, on the other hand, swimming may seem like an exhausting chore that can be done well only by people who possess a natural talent for it. The truth, however, is that anyone can learn to swim—and swim well. With this goal in mind, *Swimming: Steps to Success* shows you how to feel more comfortable in an aquatic environment and takes you through a progression of skills for each of the competitive strokes.

Step 1 starts with the basics—floating and finding your natural buoyancy. Step 2 addresses ways of manipulating the water for propulsion. Steps 3 through 6 cover the fundamentals of the four competitive strokes—freestyle, backstroke, breaststroke, and butterfly. Steps 7 and 8 focus on turns and starts, and step 9 addresses open-water and survival swimming. Step 10, the final step, gives you some guidance for continuing your swimming journey.

The *Steps to Success* approach to swimming is systematic in building on a solid foundation of skills and techniques. Each step should be approached in the following manner:

1. Carefully read all material in the step.
2. Study the technique photos and, if necessary, use a mirror or a friendly observer to duplicate them yourself.
3. Study the common errors that coaches look for so that you can avoid them!
4. When reading about and executing the drills, keep in mind that they are often designed as "overcorrections" for a specific technique flaw. Drills are intended to help you create a new pattern of movement. After completing each drill, remember to score your success.
5. At the end of each step, review the key points in the Success Summary to make sure that you understand the material. Then total your scores from the drills in that step and make sure that you've achieved the needed level of success before moving on to the next step.

As you make your way through the steps, you will begin to appreciate that swimming is not so much about brute strength as it is about the timing and rhythm of your movements. Getting it right takes a lot of thoughtful practice, and you will benefit from revisiting the steps when you have trouble with a particular skill or technique.

Swimming is a journey, and this book is designed to help you work through that journey one step at a time. Each step is laid out with a focus on a certain skills or techniques and ways to increase or decrease the difficulty. If you have trouble with a particular skill or step, remember that swimming consists of complex sets of movements that are not part of any other athletic activity. Be patient with yourself; the key is your progress. As with any journey, no matter how long or short, this one begins with the first step.

The Sport of Swimming

This book is a guide to help you better understand the fundamentals of swimming, which can be defined simply as the act of propelling oneself through the water. Because an instructional book cannot reasonably address all of the rules and regulations applied to swimming, this introduction provides an overview of the sport and introduces certain swimming terms commonly used by coaches and swimmers. Throughout the rest of the book, each term is further defined in the context in which it is typically used.

The sport of swimming has been around for thousands of years, dating back at least to 36 BCE, when Japanese people held organized swimming contests. From then right up until today, it has been a very simple matter to determine the winner of a swimming contest: whoever finishes first! Over the years, races have covered a variety of distances, ranging from about 25 yards (23 m) to lengths that could be measured in miles or kilometers.

Races can be further separated into disciplines, or strokes; they can also involve medleys, in which various strokes are used, and team relay races. In modern swimming, the strokes include freestyle (also known as the front crawl), backstroke, breaststroke, and butterfly. Modern rules dictate the specifics of format, but the essential structure of each race is the same: a start, a swim, and a finish.

THE AQUATIC ENVIRONMENT

Swimming differs from other sports in several ways. For one thing, swimming is not necessarily a natural activity for human beings. Indeed, humans bear little resemblance to species that are geared to operate in an aquatic environment; for example, fish don't have necks. As a result, in order to swim, we humans must make some adaptations—in part to accommodate our differences but also to take advantage of them.

For success in swimming, you must first become comfortable in the aquatic environment, which differs dramatically from the land-based environment in which we typically operate on a daily basis. It is easier to do so if you understand the key differences between humans and aquatic creatures. First, as mostly terrestrial creatures, we walk upright, and our natural position for most of our waking hours is basically vertical. In the water, however, most of what we do involves being horizontal, and this difference takes some getting used to for most people.

In addition, in many sports, success depends largely on strength and speed. In swimming, however, there is nothing solid to push against; therefore, though strength does matter in swimming, it is much more important to apply pressure to the water in the correct way. Because water is a fluid, it moves around you rather than resolutely resisting you in the way that a solid does. Similarly, speed in swimming comes not necessarily from moving your body parts faster but from using your movements to put pressure on the water in an effective manner. As anyone who has participated in water aerobics can attest, you can work awfully hard in the water yet go nowhere.

Swimming also changes the priorities typically placed on the human senses, as well as the feedback they provide. On land, much of our typical interaction with our environment revolves around the senses of sight and hearing. Underwater, however, both of these senses are diminished and therefore often take a backseat to the sense of touch, or "feel."

Of course, one component of this sensory feedback involves water temperature, which can greatly affect one's comfort and enjoyment when swimming. In addition, both very cold water and very hot water both pose health risks. Specifically, water temperatures below 72 degrees Fahrenheit (about 22 degrees Celsius) or above 92 degrees Fahrenheit (about 33 degrees Celsius) require special caution because they make for an uncomfortable learning environment.

Last—and this is perhaps the most striking difference between swimming and other sports—one must purposefully address the question of when (and where) to breathe. In most other sports, breathing happens without much conscious thought. In swimming, however, breathing is often a primary focus because inhaling water is not a pleasant experience. As a result, many swimmers feel that they must take a big gulp of air and then hold their breath for as long as they can while swimming. This approach typically leads to a bad experience, such as hyperventilating or even concluding that swimming is just too hard and giving up altogether.

Each of these defining characteristics of swimming is discussed in greater detail in the following chapters, which constitute a progression of steps to lead you to success!

SWIMMING VENUES: POOLS

Swimming pools come in many sizes and shapes, and various configurations can provide a great place to learn and train. Only certified pools are used in recognized competitions, and they come in a variety of strictly measured distances. In the United States, many age-group and college competitions take place in what are called short-course yard (SCY) pools, which measure 25 yards (~23 m) in length. The United States is the only country still competing in this type of pool, and other countries typically use short-course meter (SCM) pools, which measure 25 meters (~27 yd) (figure 1). Because meters are about 10 percent longer than yards, record times for meters swims are longer than those done for yard swims.

Note that in this book, yards are used for pool dimensions. If you swim in a pool measured in meters, you can use the same number given in the descriptions. For example, if an instruction is to swim 25 yards, that can also be 25 meters.

Another type of competitive swimming venue is a long-course meter (LCM) pool, which is often referred to as an Olympic-size pool. LCM pools are 50 meters (~55 yd) long, and though they may not look particularly long on Olympic television broadcasts, the experience of swimming in them can be much different than that of swimming in a short-course pool.

All of these competition pools share certain standard features, such as starting blocks and—even more important, as discussed in step 4 of this book—a set of backstroke flags. These flags, or pennants, are strung across the pool's lanes 5 yards or

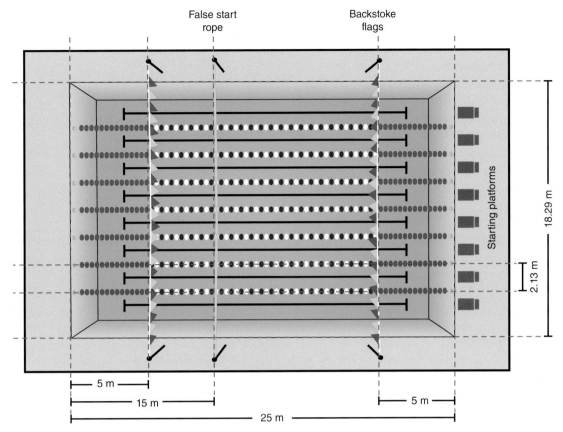

Figure 1 A 25-meter pool.

meters from the edge of the pool to signal to backstroke swimmers that they are approaching a wall—a crucial safety feature. Competition pools are also outfitted with starting blocks, or platforms. In addition, during competitions, a thin sensor is attached to the pool wall to record the time of each swimmer's first touch rather than relying on handheld timers.

POOL RACES

The majority of swimming meets and races take place in pools (rather than in open-water environments), and venues around the world host events featuring various strokes and distances on courses like those just described. Each national swimming federation has its own minor rule variations, but the basic structure of a swim race is always the same. All competitors start at the same time and adhere to the rules of the prescribed stroke, and the finish order is ranked from fastest to slowest.

In events with more participants than lanes, the competition is conducted in multiple rounds or "heats." Either heats are used to seed swimmers for the final, or heats are pregrouped to put swimmers of similar speed in the same heat, and the best time from any heat wins the race. These can be used to determine seeding for finals or so that similar-speed swimmers all swim together, and the heats are timed with the fastest swimmer being declared the winner. It has become easier to compare times from different heats thanks to the development of sophisticated timing equipment, standardized and certified pool lengths, and touch pads that automatically stop a clock when a swimmer makes contact.

GETTING STARTED: APPAREL

In order to learn the sport of swimming and train effectively for competition, you need certain kinds of gear. For starters, choosing the right suit can be an important part of both your appreciation of swimming and your comfort in the water. Many types of modern swimsuit are available in different fabrics and cuts. Something that you might wear to the beach is not necessarily the best choice for a swimming workout, since beachwear is designed more for fashion than for function. Swimsuits, on the other hand, have evolved to maximize fit and functionality.

Swimsuits

Unlike ancient swimmers, modern contestants are of course required to wear some sort of swimsuit. Suit design has changed dramatically over the years, and today males typically opt for a brief or "jammer," which runs from waist to just above the knee. These formfitting suits are typically made of a material that stretches, such as nylon, spandex, polyester, or a combination thereof. Females typically wear a one-piece suit that covers the body from the mid-thighs to the shoulders; suits vary in style and cut. For training purposes, swimmers may opt to use any of a variety of suits that are less expensive or less restrictive or provide some extra element for training purposes, such as the increased drag of looser suits.

Goggles

Goggles have been around for a long time but came into widespread use only in the 1970s; they are now considered an integral part of sport swimming. For several reasons, goggles come in many styles. How does one know which style to buy? Some styles are geared toward a particular activity, such as scuba diving, snorkeling, or triathlon, and others are available in different sizes, shapes, and tints.

Quality should be assessed on the basis not of price but of fit. The best goggles are the ones that fit *you*—that is, the ones that fit your face comfortably and keep the water out. Remember, their purpose is to enhance your vision and reduce eye irritation from pool chemicals or, in open-water environments, other sources. To test the fit, place the eyepieces on your eye sockets, below the bony part where the eyebrows are located, in the softer part of each socket. Without using the strap, press the goggles gently onto this soft tissue and see if they stay even for just a few seconds; if they do, you have a good fit! The strap merely needs to hold the goggles in place, and of course it should not be made so tight as to injure your eyes. The strap should fit above your ears and wrap near the top of the back of your head (not at the base of your skull down near your neck).

Beyond these basics, goggle preference is an individual matter, much like the choice of putter for a golfer. Considerations include one's face shape and head size, as well as one's preference for a foam, silicone, or rubber gasket (or no gasket at all). The gasket is simply the part of the goggle that contacts the face around the eye or the barrier between plastic and your face. Choosing among these options is largely a matter of what works best for you. Most sporting goods stores and swimming pro shops carry a variety of goggles, and you can simply ask an associate for a demo model or for permission to open a package in order to check the fit.

Caps

A swimmer with long hair often wears a cap for two reasons. First, of course, it keeps the hair out of the way and reduces drag; second, it provides a measure of protection from the sometimes-harsh chemicals or other environmental factors in the water. These environmental factors can include the sun when outside, bacteria in the water, and other chemicals in the water—such as a residual-like suntan lotion that came off other swimmers, runoff from chemicals on the deck when it rains, or other chemicals from pollution that can be found in open-water environments. Swim caps are made often of latex, silicone, or (for very cold water) neoprene; they vary in style and price. If you decide to wear a cap, take care to choose one that works for you. Cap sizing tends to be one-size-fits-all, but small differences do exist from brand to brand. Keep in mind that, like rubber bands, caps can stretch and break; they typically include a care-and-use guide in their packaging.

GETTING STARTED: TRAINING EQUIPMENT

In swimming, training equipment is often used to conduct drills and improve swimming-specific movements by increasing resistance. It can also serve as an assistive device that enables swimmers to isolate a specific movement or set of skills. Such equipment is not necessary for the sport, but it can make many skills and drills easier to master and perfect. At many facilities, equipment is made available to patrons, thus enabling you to test out the gear and learn what to look for if you choose to purchase your own. Common equipment used in swimming includes kickboards, fins, paddles, pull buoys, and snorkels.

Kickboards

The kickboard (figure 2) is a fairly common piece of equipment found in many swimmers' training bags. It is typically made of some sort of foam to provide flotation. Its purpose is to provide a buoyancy assist so that swimmers can isolate and train the kicking motion. It is often used to train all four competitive strokes.

Figure 2 Two different styles of kickboards.

Fins

Fins are commonly used in swim training to add resistance to the kicking motion, helping the person to swim more easily or to make the workout harder. They come in a variety of shapes and sizes (figure 3), and some are designed specifically for a certain competitive stroke—for example, the monofin and the breaststroke fin. Monofins are a training tool specific to dolphin kick. Breaststroke fins are also very specific to that kick and, due to the increase in pressure on the groin area and the inside of the knee, should probably be used only under the supervision of a knowledgeable coach and with a swimmer who has had sufficient technique training and the strength to benefit from the extra resistance. For training purposes, fins with medium-size blades work for most swimmers, though it is a good idea to use shorter blades in the beginning in order to prevent injury. People who have less strength or flexibility in the lower extremities—especially the ankles—should definitely use a medium or shorter blade of 6 to 9 inches (about 15 to 23 centimeters) to prevent overstressing those joints with the added pressure and resistance created by longer blades (often seen in scuba shops). In addition, short-blade fins (shorter than 6 inches, or 15 centimeters) are often used to work with just a little extra resistance while maintaining kicking cadence and rhythm. As with goggles, fit is very important. A good fit is not too tight or loose, and some swimmers prefer a sock as it makes the fin more comfortable. This is very similar to trying on shoes.

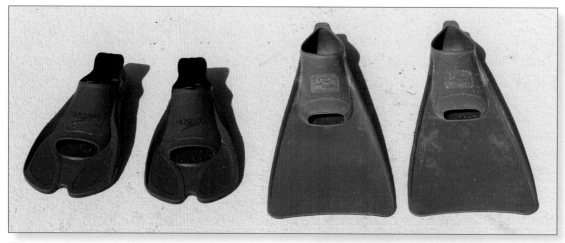

Figure 3   Fins of various lengths.

Paddles

Like goggles and fins, paddles for swimming come in a variety of shapes and sizes (figure 4). Paddles are often used to create extra resistance by increasing the surface area of the hands. As with fins, great care should be taken when using paddles because the increased pressure on the water creates extra stress on the joints—in this case the shoulders. As a result, novices should use smaller paddles in order to minimize the risk of injury.

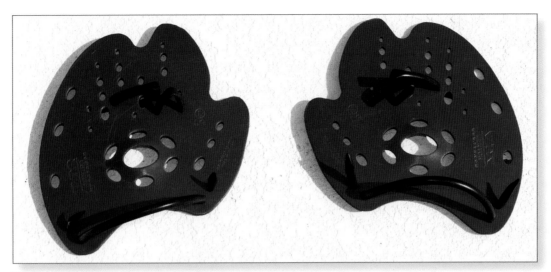

Figure 4 Paddles. Sizes and shapes vary widely depending on manufacturer and purpose.

Pull Buoys

A pull buoy (figure 5) is fitted between the thighs, just above the knees, and the swimmer keeps it in place by squeezing the thighs together. This arrangement prevents the swimmer from using any effective kick in the freestyle or backstroke, thus isolating and training the pulling motion of the swimming arm stroke.

Figure 5 Pull bouys. Size and shape will vary from manufacturer to manufacturer.

Snorkel

The swimmer's snorkel is a fairly recent development (figure 6). Of course, traditional side-mounted snorkels have been around for years, but the newer center-mounted snorkel is designed specifically for swim training. It allows swimmers to focus fully on their strokes without the added concern of when and where to breathe.

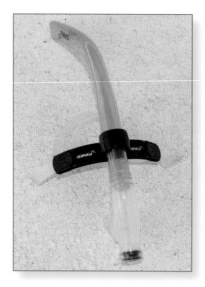

Figure 6   Swimmers' snorkels are typically center mounted rather than offset like they are for scuba diving, and they have a strap that goes around the head.

GETTING STARTED: DRILLS AND THEIR PURPOSE

Because body movements are controlled by the brain, the activity of swimming—an unnatural activity for humans that requires complex, timed movements—requires us to program the brain in order to direct the body effectively in the water. This process is sometimes referred to as developing "muscle memory," but it actually involves brain imprinting and patterning. With this in mind, several drills are described for each step in this book in order to imprint the relevant movement patterns on your brain so that you can easily replicate them over and over again. One caveat: Some of the drills imprint an overcorrection that will later be refined.

As mentioned earlier, swimmers often use training equipment to help them acquire new skills or imprint new movement patterns. One must also take care, however, not to become dependent on that equipment for being able to move through the water with skill and ease. In addition, your success depends on doing the drills and using the equipment correctly rather than quickly. As with any learning, some swimmers progress faster than others, and each skill presents new a challenge. Therefore, prepare yourself to be patient—swimming is a learned process that takes some time.

Swimming is one of the best sports in which to participate from a very young age to a very old age. Some competitions even offer a 95-and-over age group! Athletes can participate in this sport for such a long time—and at such advanced ages—because of its low- to no-impact nature and the fact that it enables one to focus on technique and effective movement. Science tells us that at a certain point in life we stop getting stronger and gaining endurance; however, even though you may not be able to get faster after a certain point, swimming always gives you a chance to get *better*.

Let's move on now to the steps to swimming success, which enable you to learn and practice skills that provide a solid foundation for lifelong enjoyment!

Floating

The goal of this first step is to move from a vertical position to the horizontal neutral position that serves as the platform for swimming in all four competitive strokes. This step also helps you become comfortable in the water. By the end of this step, you should be able to

- transition from vertical to floating on your back,
- transition from vertical to floating on your front,
- balance on your center of buoyancy in a streamlined position on your back, and
- balance on your center of buoyancy in a streamlined position on your front.

THE PHYSICS OF BUOYANCY AND FLOATING

Floating is a skill, which means that anyone can do it if he or she learns how. As humans, we float naturally, at least to some degree, because our lungs are filled with air. In fact, our center of buoyancy is located approximately in the center of the chest, at the sternum. Some other sports also require attention to one's center of gravity, but the priority in swimming, of course, is to find that center while moving through the water.

You can imagine this center as the center of a teeter-totter or seesaw on a children's playground. When everything is in balance, the teeter-totter does not move. Lift either end, however, and the opposite end goes down. With this analogy in mind, you can start learning how to float on your back.

FLOATING ON YOUR BACK

This section takes you from standing in a vertical position to simply floating on your back. You need access to a pool with water deep enough to reach at least to your waist but shallow enough that you can still stand in it. If needed, the action can also be done from the side of a deep pool with a few modifications.

Back Floating With Arms Extended

The objective here is to lie back on the water with your arms and legs spread out for balance, almost like a starfish, and float without movement (figure 1.1). Before you try it, here are a couple of mental cues to help you quickly succeed. The first cue addresses head position. Imagine having a dot on the top of your head that must stay wet. Many swimmers are uncomfortable having the head so far in the water, especially when water goes into the ears, but the water *will* come back out!

The second cue addresses body position. The goal is to keep your spine as elongated and horizontal as possible. If you feel your feet sink, do not crunch with your abs but rather push your navel to the top of the water. Some swimmers also find it helpful to close their eyes in order to concentrate on how it feels to balance in the water. Remember the teeter-totter—the minute you lift your head, your hips go down.

Figure 1.1 BACK FLOATING WITH ARMS EXTENDED

Preparation

1. Begin by checking the water around you to ensure that you have enough room to perform the skill.
2. To help with balance, move your arms and legs out and away from your body.

Execution

1. From the standing position, lean your head back and lie back on the water.
2. It is helpful to push off of the bottom to get your feet up. It may be necessary to use a kicking motion, or a sculling-and-sweeping motion with your hands, to get to a horizontal position.
3. Lie still on the water with your face, chest, hips, and toes all on the surface.

MISSTEP

Your feet sink.

CORRECTION

Push your back toward the bottom of the pool and your hips up. Be sure that your neck is relaxed and your head is back.

MISSTEP

Your hips sink.

CORRECTION

Ensure that your abs are not contracted (as in doing crunches); this part of your body should be relaxed. Make sure that there is no tension in the front of your neck from lifting your head.

MISSTEP

Your head and feet are both underwater.

CORRECTION

This problem results from arching the back too much. Keep your spine straight and your limbs relaxed and out to the sides rather for balance. Once you are able to do this successfully for at least a few seconds, it is time to move on to more advanced floating skills.

Back Floating in a T Position

The next part of this progression involves taking away some of the surfaces that swimmers use for balance. Repeat the same skill just described, but this time keep your arms out while bringing your legs together, thus making a T rather than a starfish (figure 1.2). This action requires a little more control and ability to relax on the water. Here again, the mental cue is that your face, chest, hips, and toes should all be at the surface—only this time they should also all be in the same line along the axis of your body.

Figure 1.2 **BACK FLOATING IN A T POSITION**

Preparation

1. Begin by checking the water around you to ensure that you have enough room to perform the skill.
2. To help with balance, move your arms and legs out and away from your body.

Execution

1. From a standing position, lean your head back and lie back on the water.
2. It is helpful to push off of the bottom to get your feet up. It may be necessary to use a kicking motion, or a sculling-and-sweeping motion with your hands, to get to a horizontal position.
3. Lie still on the water with your face, chest, hips, and toes all on the surface.
4. Form a T position by extending your arms to your sides, perpendicular to your body, while keeping your legs straight.

MISSTEP

You have to move your arms to stay afloat.

CORRECTION

Think about pushing your hips up and pulling your belly button toward your spine. This will orient your body for better buoyancy.

Back Floating in a Straight Line

The last part of this progression involves bringing your hands in to the sides of your body. As you become more comfortable with this balanced position, you can try a more advanced floating technique. From your sides, bring your hands up above your head, stretching to the longest possible position (figure 1.3). This is a more advanced floating skill, and succeeding at it is a major accomplishment; in fact, some people who have difficulty mastering it still go on to become very accomplished swimmers. Once you have mastered these skills, it is time to practice them with modifications and drills.

Figure 1.3   **BACK FLOATING IN A STRAIGHT LINE**

Preparation

1. Begin by checking the water around you to ensure that you have enough room to perform the skill.
2. To help with balance, move your arms and legs out and away from your body.

Execution

1. From the standing position, lean your head back and lie back on the water.
2. It is helpful to push off of the bottom to get the feet up. It may be necessary to use a kicking motion, or a sculling-and-sweeping motion with your hands, to get to a horizontal position.
3. Lie still on the water with your face, chest, hips, and toes all on the surface.
4. Extend the arms above the head and stretch to the longest position possible.

MISSTEP

Your upper body and chest are floating, but your feet are sinking.

CORRECTION

Many people arch the back to push the torso up. Push the upper part of the back down and rotate the pelvis up to bring the feet up to the surface of the water. It may be helpful to visualize bringing the belly button closer to the spine.

DRILLS FOR PRACTICING BACK FLOATING

Just as basketball players don't shoot one free throw and assume they have mastered the skill, swimmers practice their techniques over and over—even the basic ones—to keep their skills sharp. Once you feel comfortable that you are able to perform this skill floating on the back, it is time to practice it without assistance from the bottom of the pool. To practice going from vertical to horizontal, use the following series of drills. They can be performed in deep water if you are comfortable in that environment and possess at least a beginning level of swimming skill. Otherwise, do them in water no deeper than neck level.

Back-Floating Drill 1   Push-Off on Your Back

In this drill, you are positioned at the side of the pool, facing the wall, with both hands on the gutter or deck. Your feet should be on the wall and your knees and toes pointing up toward the surface of the water. Lean your head back (looking up), release your hands from the side of the pool, gently push off with your feet, and assume a relaxed floating position.

For many swimmers, this drill requires more than one try. Here is the sequence once again: lean head back, release hands, and gently push off with feet. You have succeeded when you can do the drill repeatedly with your legs together and your arms crossed. The purpose of this drill is to help you get skilled at and comfortable with going from a semivertical position to a horizontal back float.

TO INCREASE DIFFICULTY

• Push off harder.

TO DECREASE DIFFICULTY

• Have your coach or instructor hold your head to ensure that it stays above the water.

• Keep your arms at your sides or out perpendicular to the body.

• Hold a kickboard across your chest.

Success Check

- You can push off and maintain a balanced position.
- You can stay in the balanced position for more than 20 seconds.

Score Your Success

1 point: You can float on the water with your arms out.

3 points: You can push off of the wall gently and hold the balanced position for 5 seconds with your arms out.

5 points: You can push off of the wall gently and hold the balanced position for 10 seconds with your arms at your sides.

7 points: You can push off of the wall gently and hold the balanced position for 20 seconds or more with your arms crossed or at your sides.

Back-Floating Drill 2   Position

This drill is a variation of the previous drill. This time, pick up your feet rather than pushing off of the bottom of the pool; alternatively, you can tread water if you are performing the drill from a vertical position in a deep pool.

The drill consists of starting vertical and achieving a horizontal back float, then lifting your head and returning to vertical. It helps you achieve the horizontal back float and attend to how your head position affects your body position. Returning to the teeter-totter analogy, when one end (your head) goes up, the other end (your hips) goes down. Practice this drill several times in order to develop a good sense of balance.

TO INCREASE DIFFICULTY

- Use only a kicking motion with your legs or your hands to manipulate your position in the water, but not both.

TO DECREASE DIFFICULTY

- Use both your arms and your legs.

Back-Floating Drill 3   Touch Your Nose

This drill builds on the skill of floating on the water in a T position. Assume the horizontal back-float position with your arms straight out to your sides, then touch your nose with an index finger while continuing to float. Repeat with the index finger of the opposite hand. This more advanced drill helps you develop not only vertical and horizontal balance but also lateral or side-to-side balance. As you get the hang of it, try passing a tennis ball from one hand to the other while maintaining your balance.

(continued)

Back-Floating Drill 3 *(continued)*

TO INCREASE DIFFICULTY

• Do the drill in deep water.

TO DECREASE DIFFICULTY

• Have your coach or instructor hold your head to ensure that it stays above the water.
• Keep your arms at your sides or out perpendicular to the body.
• Hold a kickboard across your chest.

Success Check

• You can go from vertical to horizontal and maintain a balanced position.
• You can stay in the balanced position for more than 20 seconds.

Score Your Success

1 point: You can float on the water with your arms crossed.

3 points: You can push off of the wall gently and hold the balanced position for 5 seconds.

5 points: You can push off of the wall gently and hold the balanced position for 10 seconds.

7 points: You can push off of the wall gently and hold the balanced position for 20 seconds or more.

FLOATING ON YOUR FRONT

The next skill in this step involves floating on your front. This is essentially the same skill as floating on your back—and the same physics apply—but with the added element that your face is in the water. As a result, you can practice two skills at once: floating and exhaling with your face in the water.

Front Floating With Arms Extended

From a standing position in the water, lie on the water in a position not unlike the starfish discussed earlier. The objective here is to keep your head, shoulders, hips, hands, and feet all at the surface of the water (figure 1.4).

You can try this first exercise while holding your breath. One indicator of success is being able to look straight down at the bottom of the pool while relaxing on the water in a horizontal position with your back straight. After you become comfortable in this position, try it again—only this time breathe out slowly. Breath holding causes tension, which can lead a swimmer to sink or struggle with balance; exhaling slowly, on the other hand, aids relaxation and is also a necessary skill for performing the competitive strokes. To control your breathing, rather than exhaling forcefully, breathe out through your nose while humming.

Figure 1.4 **FRONT FLOATING WITH ARMS EXTENDED**

Preparation

1. Begin by checking the water around you to ensure that you have enough room to perform the skill.
2. To help with balance, move your arms and legs out and away from your body.

Execution

1. From the standing position, lean forward and lie facedown on the water.
2. It is helpful to push off of the bottom to get the feet up. It may be necessary to use a kicking motion, or a sculling-and-sweeping motion with your hands, to get to a horizontal position.
3. Lie still on the water with your head, back, hips, and heels all on the surface.

MISSTEP

Your feet sink.

CORRECTION

Push your chest toward the bottom of the pool and your hips up. Be sure that your neck is relaxed and your head is in line with your spine. For a good mental image, imagine stretching your neck and making it very long.

MISSTEP

Your hips sink.

CORRECTION

Ensure that your abs are not contracted (as in doing crunches); this part of your body should be relaxed. Make sure that there is no tension in the back of your neck from lifting your head.

MISSTEP

Your head and feet are underwater.

CORRECTION

This problem result comes from curling the back too much. Keep your spine straight and your limbs relaxed and out away from the body for balance. Once you are able to perform this skill successfully for at least a few seconds, it is time to move on to more advanced floating skills.

Front Floating in a T Position

The next part of this progression takes away some of the surfaces that swimmers use for balance. As with floating on your back, the next skill to master is floating on your front while bringing your legs together. Specifically, repeat the same skill, but this time keep your arms out while bringing your legs together to make a T rather than a starfish (figure 1.5). This skill requires a little more control and ability to relax on the water.

Figure 1.5 **FRONT FLOATING IN A T POSITION**

Preparation

1. Begin by checking the water around you to ensure that you have enough room to perform the skill.
2. To help with balance, move your arms and legs out and away from your body.

Execution

1. From the standing position, lean forward and lie facedown on the water.
2. It is helpful to push off of the bottom to get the feet up. It may be necessary to use a kicking motion, or a sculling-and-sweeping motion with your hands, to get to a horizontal position.
3. Lie still on the water with your head, back, hips, and heels all on the surface.
4. Bring your legs together to form a T shape on the water.

MISSTEP

Your feet are sinking.

CORRECTION

Check your head position. If it is looking forward, then lengthen the neck and look straight down.

Front Floating in a Straight Line

The last part of this progression involves bringing your hands in front of your body (figure 1.6). As before, imagine your face, chest, hips, and heels all at the surface—only now they are also in the same line down the axis of your body. Once again, you can try this skill while holding your breath until you have a stable floating position, then slowly exhale. You may feel a little like you are sinking as you exhale due to the change in the volume of air in your lungs. This is a more advanced floating skill, and succeeding at it is a major accomplishment; at the same time, most swimmers find it easier than doing the same thing on the back.

Figure 1.6 FRONT FLOATING IN A STRAIGHT LINE

Preparation

1. Begin by checking the water around you to ensure that you have enough room to perform the skill.
2. To help with balance, move your arms and legs out and away from your body.

Execution

1. Bring your hands in front of your body.
2. Place each hand on the opposite shoulder with your arms crossed on your chest.

MISSTEP

Your feet sink even though your hands are keeping you balanced.

CORRECTION

Check to make sure you are not hunching your back. Press your chest toward the bottom of the pool and bring your hips up.

DRILLS FOR PRACTICING FRONT FLOATING

As you have learned by now, floating on the front is fundamentally different from floating on the back. Because of being facedown rather than faceup, you do not have the freedom to breathe whenever you want to. The key to becoming comfortable in the facedown position is to practice certain drills, which can move you toward being as comfortable in this position as you are on your back.

Front-Floating Drill 1   Push-Off

Stand at the side of the pool, sink under the water, and draw your feet up to the wall. Next, push off horizontally and work to rise to the surface and float horizontally, as before, by lying on the water. For many swimmers, this drill requires more than one try. Here is the sequence once again: sink under the water, draw your feet up to the wall, and gently push off with your feet. You have succeeded when you can do the drill repeatedly with your legs together and your arms crossed. The purpose of this drill is to help you get skilled at and comfortable with going from an underwater position to a horizontal front float.

TO INCREASE DIFFICULTY

- Push off harder.
- Hold your arms above your head.

TO DECREASE DIFFICULTY

- Have your coach or instructor assist you by holding your hands out in front of you above your head.
- Keep your arms at your sides.
- Hold a kickboard across your chest.

Success Check

- You can push off and maintain a balanced position.
- You can push off and maintain a balanced position for more than 20 seconds.

Score Your Success

1 point: You can float on the water with your arms crossed.

3 points: You can push off of the wall gently and hold the balanced position for 5 seconds.

5 points: You can push off of the wall gently and hold the balanced position for 10 seconds.

7 points: You can push off of the wall gently and hold the balanced position for 20 seconds or more.

Front-Floating Drill 2   Position

This drill is a variation of drill 2 for the back float. This time, pick up your feet rather than pushing off of the bottom of the pool; alternatively, you can tread water if you are performing the drill from a vertical position in a deep pool. Perform this drill by curling up into a tuck or ball position, then spreading out and trying to achieve the front floating position. This drill also helps you prepare for step 2 of this book, which addresses how to manipulate the water.

TO INCREASE DIFFICULTY

- Push off harder.
- Hold your hands above your head.

TO DECREASE DIFFICULTY

- Have your coach or instructor assist by holding the head or the hands steady.
- Keep your arms at your sides or out perpendicular to the body.
- Hold a kickboard across your chest.

Success Check

- You can push off and maintain a balanced position.
- You can push off and maintain a balanced position for more than 20 seconds.

Score Your Success

1 point: You can float on the water with your arms crossed.

3 points: You can push off of the wall gently and hold the balanced position for 5 seconds.

5 points: You can push off of the wall gently and hold the balanced position for 10 seconds.

7 points: You can push off of the wall gently and hold the balanced position for 20 seconds or more.

Front-Floating Drill 3   *Horizontal Jumping Jacks*

This drill builds on the skill of lying on the water in a starfish position. Here, you alternate moving your hands and feet with your hands above your head and your legs spread with your hands out and your body in a T position. Try this both on your back and on your front. The movement should be done very slowly and should mimic the classic jumping-jack exercise. This drill helps you master the balancing forces and find your center of buoyancy.

TO INCREASE DIFFICULTY

- Move your arms and legs in a way that propels you forward.

TO DECREASE DIFFICULTY

- Have your coach or instructor hold your head to ensure that it stays above the water.
- Move just your arms or your legs.

Success Check

- You can push off and maintain a balanced position.
- You can push off and maintain a balanced, horizontal position while moving both your arms and your legs.

Score Your Success

1 point: You can float on the water and move just your arms or your legs.

3 points: You can float on the water and move both your arms and your legs, but only once.

5 points: You can float on the water and move both your arms and your legs multiple times.

7 points: You can perform the drill and move forward.

THE SWIMMING POSITION

The last skills in this step involve using your newfound balance in the water to achieve a swimming position and to master the art of reducing drag force. A good swimming position requires a great deal of balance and a solid foundation that enables you to apply force to the water. As discussed earlier, it is critical to locate your center of balance and be comfortable in the water.

Return for a moment to the teeter-totter analogy and the fact that your center of buoyancy lies in the middle of your chest. If you stand poolside with your arms at your sides, about two-thirds of your personal teeter-totter—that is, everything from your chest to your feet—lies below your center of buoyancy. In order to achieve a good swimming position, you need to bring the teeter-totter back into balance. To that end, as soon as you raise your arms above your head, about half of your length is above your center of buoyancy and the other half is below it. There is a time when the body is extended in this fashion in each of the four competitive strokes.

Finding Your Balance on Your Back

If starting with the back float, the objective is to raise your arms above your head and stretch them as far as you can. Be as long as you can from fingertips to toe tips and still maintain a good floating position. Note that in this position, you have very few ways to manipulate the water for lateral balance. Learning balance in this position can prove challenging for people with limited flexibility or limited range of motion in the shoulders. You have succeeded when you can maintain a relaxed floating position with your hands extended beyond your head. Use the following steps to find your balance while floating on your back.

PREPARATION

1. Begin by checking the water around you to ensure that you have enough room to perform the skill.
2. To help with balance, move your arms and legs out away from your body.
3. Hold your fingers tightly together on both hands.

EXECUTION

1. Lie on your back with your arms extended above your head.
2. Stretch your arms to the longest position from fingertips to toes.
3. Make adjustments to the position of your upper back and hips to ensure that the hands, shoulders, hips, and toes are all at the top of the water.

Streamlined Floating on Your Back

The next skill in floating on your back is to establish a streamlined position (figure 1.7)—one in which you are not only as long as you can be (from fingertips to toe tips) but also as skinny as possible. This streamlining reduces drag force (discussed in step 2) and sets you up to move through the water more effectively in later stages of the learning process. A good streamline involves certain key elements—extending the body into a line as long as possible from fingertips to toe tips, keeping the core tight, and making yourself as skinny as possible—starting at the fingertips and working down from there.

Figure 1.7 STREAMLINED FLOATING ON YOUR BACK

Preparation

1. Begin by checking the water around you to ensure that you have enough room to perform the skill.
2. To help with balance, move your arms and legs out and away from your body.
3. Hold your fingers tightly together on both hands.

Execution

1. From the standing position, lean your head back and lie back on the water.
2. Lie still on the water with your face, chest, hips, and toes all on the surface.
3. As you work your way down, checking to make sure everything is streamlined, your hands should be stacked, one on top of the other. For now, it does not matter which hand is on top, but the thumb of your top hand should wrap under your bottom hand just a little to lock your hands into place.
4. Stretch out so that your toes are pointed and your arms are squeezing your ears.

MISSTEP

Your elbows are bent.

CORRECTION

For most people, the simple cue "squeeze your ears with your arms" is effective. People with more flexibility can put their elbows behind the head and try to squeeze the forearms completely together.

As just mentioned in streamlined floating, head position depends on flexibility. Your torso should be straight, and a good visual for this element is to imagine keeping your spine as long as possible; this image helps you keep your head and torso in line. Your legs should be closed completely and together all the way through, with even your big toes connected. Your feet and toes should be pointed much like those of a ballet dancer; the exact degree of angle depends on the flexibility of your ankles.

Streamlined Floating on Your Front

The streamline on the front (figure 1.8) is produced in the same manner as on the back; it is more challenging, however, because your face is in the water. In both positions, success is measured by how well you maintain both the horizontal position in the water and the long, stretched-out position with no movement.

Figure 1.8 **STREAMLINED FLOATING ON YOUR FRONT**

Preparation

1. From the standing position, lean forward and lie facedown on the water.
2. To help with balance, move your arms and legs out and away from your body.

Execution

1. Extend your arms and legs on the same line to make yourself as long as you can from fingertips to toe tips.
2. Stretch out so that your toes are pointed and your arms are squeezing your ears.

DRILLS FOR AN EFFECTIVE STREAMLINE

Streamlining is often referred to as the fifth stroke. Its purpose is to set up a good swimming position and minimize the drag force that slows you down and makes it harder to perform each movement. You will learn more about streamlining in later steps; for now, here are some drills to help you begin to master it.

Streamline Drill 1   Shadow Streamlines

This drill is done out of the pool and is good for both front and back streamlines. Perform this drill on a sunny day on a pool deck, either next to a wall or in a location where you can see your shadow on the deck. Assume the streamlined position as described earlier and look at your shadow for visual feedback. Try different ways of making your shadow as narrow as possible.

TO INCREASE DIFFICULTY

- Look at the streamline both from the side and from the front. This adjusts positions of the torso from different views. Wide in one plane can be thin in another. Finding the balance of both planes is more advanced.

TO DECREASE DIFFICULTY

- Use a full-length mirror. This can be done anywhere, not just in the bright sunshine.

Success Check

- You can see the difference in your width when you go from standing with your arms at your sides to a streamlined position.

Score Your Success

1 point: You can do the drill with a mirror.

3 points: You can do the drill on the pool deck.

Streamline Drill 2   Pencil to a Brick

This drill emphasizes the importance of the streamline. Sink under the water and assume the streamlined position with your feet on the wall. Push off forcefully and then, after moving just a few feet, spread your arms and legs apart to make a brick. You will feel yourself come almost immediately to a stop! Try it a few times and note where in the pool you stop.

TO INCREASE DIFFICULTY

- Push off harder, count to two, and then go to the brick position.

TO DECREASE DIFFICULTY

- Start on top of the water.

Success Check

- You can push off and glide until you stop.
- You can come to a complete stop after going to the brick position.

Score Your Success

1 point: You can push off but don't go far, even without the brick position.

3 points: You can push off and go 5 yards or more before stopping.

5 points: You can push off and go 5 yards or more before going to the brick position to stop.

Streamline Drill 3   Torpedo

This drill complements the pencil-to-brick drill. Here, you sink under the water, assume the streamlined position, push off forcefully, and, without making any other movements, see how far you go before stopping. This drill gives you an idea of the importance of reducing drag force. Remember, in the streamlined position, your hands are stacked and your arms are squeezing your ears (or head under and squeezing your elbows together); your legs are long and your toes pointed.

TO INCREASE DIFFICULTY

- Push off harder.

TO DECREASE DIFFICULTY

- Stay on top of the water.

Success Check

- You can push off and streamline for several yards underwater.
- You can stay in the streamlined position until you come to a complete stop.

Score Your Success

1 point: You can streamline for 5 yards.

3 points: You can streamline for 10 yards.

5 points: You can streamline for 12.5 yards.

7 points: You can streamline for more than 12.5 yards.

SUCCESS SUMMARY

In this step, you have learned about the foundations of good swimming with floating and buoyancy. More specifically, you have learned and practiced drills that create a solid foundation for swimming and for applying force to the water in order to move through it efficiently. You have also learned about the importance of using the streamlined position to reduce drag.

In addition, the drills and skills included in this step have led you to be more comfortable in the water, especially in positions that are not natural in most of your nonaquatic life. Being relaxed and comfortable is a key factor in the remaining steps to swimming success. You are well on your way to success in swimming if you have mastered the following skills:

1. Transitioning from a vertical position to floating on your back
2. Transitioning from a vertical position to floating on your front
3. Balancing on your center of buoyancy in a streamlined position on your back
4. Balancing on your center of buoyancy in a streamlined position on your front

SCORE YOUR SUCCESS

If you scored more than 30 points, then you have completed this step. If you scored more than 40 points, then you have mastered buoyancy and aquatic positions.

Back-Floating Drills—Vertical to Horizontal

1.	Push-Off on Your Back	_____ out of 7
2.	Position	_____ out of 7
3.	Touch Your Nose	_____ out of 7

Front-Floating Drills—Vertical to Horizontal

1.	Push-Off	_____ out of 7
2.	Position	_____ out of 7
3.	Horizontal Jumping Jacks	_____ out of 7

Streamline Drills

1.	Shadow Streamlines	_____ out of 3
2.	Pencil to a Brick	_____ out of 5
3.	Torpedo	_____ out of 7
	Total	**_____ out of 57**

In step 2, you will learn motions that put pressure on the water and movements that impede motion in the water. Some of the drills do not resemble swimming, but they show you how manipulating your body position and putting pressure on the water in different ways can help you achieve your goal of success in swimming!

Manipulating the Water

The goal of this second step is to increase your awareness of drag force, propulsive force, and how specific movements create propulsion and minimize drag. In other words, this step helps you understand how to use your body's surfaces to apply pressure on the water in order to move through it. By the end of this step, you should be able to

- achieve an aquatic position that minimizes drag;
- get a feel for the water and where it slips off of your hands when anchoring your hands during the crucial catch phase of a stroke;
- use a sculling motion for propulsion; and
- use flutter, dolphin, and breaststroke kicks for propulsion, both on your back and on your front.

DRAG FORCE AND PROPULSIVE FORCE

Drag force slows you down, whereas propulsive force makes you move. Drag force is easy to understand if you think in terms of skydiving. While falling, skydivers accelerate due to gravity. They accelerate more if they make themselves skinny and vertical (i.e., streamlined), thereby minimizing their cross-sectional area (the area facing in their direction of travel) and in turn minimizing the resistance or drag force that acts on them. On the other hand, if they spread their arms and legs out and become more horizontal, they maximize the area that is perpendicular to their direction of fall and thus slow down due to air resistance. At some point, our daredevils deploy their parachutes, greatly increasing their cross-sectional area, in order to slow down even more and avoid plummeting to their doom.

What does this have to do with swimming? Aerodynamics and hydrodynamics have a lot in common! The big difference lies in the fact that water is about 750 times denser than air and therefore involves much higher drag force. This strong resistance is the reason that high divers can slow down so quickly upon entering the water even at very high speeds. Of course, it also slows down swimmers.

At the same time, however, water gives swimmers a denser surface upon which to apply pressure than air does. Swimmers can take advantage of this density by using propulsive force to their advantage. Specifically, they apply pressure to the water in a direction that is perpendicular to the direction in which they want to go. Think of it this way: When you exit the pool, you place your hands on the pool deck in a horizontal position—that is, perpendicular to the direction (up) in which you want to go. As you apply pressure downward, your body rises above the position where it started. Now, mentally rotate these dynamics from the vertical to the horizontal and envision pressing against water instead of against the pool deck, and you have the basic concept of using propulsive force for swimming.

For another analogy, consider rockets, which are powered by massive propulsive force and resisted by relatively little drag force because they are long and skinny. Similarly, as discussed in step 1 of this book, a swimmer is well advised to assume a long, thin shape with good balance. Here in step 2, it is time to apply propulsive force. Now that you have reduced drag force by becoming streamlined, you can move on to using propulsive force by putting pressure on the water in an appropriate way.

MINIMIZING DRAG

Learning to minimize your "drag profile" takes repetition and some minor adjustments. As in step 1, in which you achieved balance in a streamlined position, you now start by ensuring that you are as long and narrow (i.e., as rocketlike) as possible. In order to feel the effects of drag and minimize their influence, repeat the push-off drill but add some new elements, starting with the manner in which you push off. The following few instructions provide a sequence that not only helps you understand how drag affects swimming but also reinforces your ability to balance in the water (figure 2.1). For the first part of this sequence, position yourself in shallow water at the pool wall. This is the only time in the sequence that you will get to push against something solid, so make it count!

TIPS FOR MINIMIZING DRAG

1. Posture is important. Make yourself as long as you can, from fingertips to toe tips. Doing so includes really stretching and pointing your toes!

2. Avoid the "Superman flying position" in which your hands are separated and your arms are parallel to each other. If you are trying to be narrow, stack your hands one on top of the other as in the Torpedo drill in step 1. A point at the front and at the back is best. Hydrodynamics tells us that you want to be long and skinny so pierce the water and let it flow off a single point at the end as well.

3. Your head is your rudder. If you keep your head down and your neck long, you will go farther. This position is also worth practicing for another reason: it is not far from your ideal front-swimming position.

Figure 2.1 **MINIMIZING DRAG**

Preparation

1. In shallow water, stand on the pool bottom while facing the wall.
2. Place both hands on the deck or gutter for balance.
3. Bring your feet up and plant them flat on the wall about two feet (0.6 m) below the surface of the water, or even with your hips, with your knees bent at about 90 degrees. Be sure that your feet are as close to flat as possible on the wall.
4. In this position—with your head up, knees up (pointing upward), and toes up—you should still be facing the wall.

Execution

1. While still facing the wall, release one hand and point it down the pool lane under the water. Doing so causes a slight twist in your hips and more in your shoulders.
2. Release the wall with your other hand and wait to sink below the water while bringing your hands together.
3. When your head, hands, hips, and feet are all at the same level under the water, push off forcefully and make your body as narrow as possible. Use the same position as described in step 1: hand on top of hand, arms squeezing your ears, core tight, and toes pointed.
4. Glide without movement as far as you can.
5. Repeat the process several times with the goal of going farther each time.

MISSTEP

You never get under the water.

CORRECTION

Everyone sinks at some point; this is simply a matter of timing. Wait until your hands touch underwater and you are completely submerged, *then* push.

MISSTEP

You spear up quickly through the top of the water.

CORRECTION

Think about where your head is. This misstep is likely to occur if you look at your hands during the push-off. If you look down at the pool bottom or even tuck your chin to your chest, you will be able to stay under.

MISSTEP

You don't go very far.

CORRECTION

Distance traveled differs from person to person. We come in different sizes and shapes, and some swimmers will go farther than others. Keep at it, and those little adjustments will make a difference!

PROPULSIVE FORCE: DEVELOPING THE CATCH AND THE PULL

Swim coaches regularly use the terms *catch* and *pull*. Roughly, *catch* means where you anchor your hand or any other frontal surface in the water; it applies to all strokes. *Pull* refers to the motion that comes immediately after the catch to provide propulsive force. In this step, you work on the general feeling of putting pressure on the water but not on the specific movement patterns for each stroke. That work comes in later steps.

THE CATCH

Manipulating the water across all strokes is a key to good swimming. As part of this process, all strokes include a catch phase (figure 2.2), in which the key surface (whether in the form of one hand or both hands) enters the water and begins to get perpendicular to the direction in which you are going. For a mental representation of the catch phase, swimmers think about anchoring the hand in the water, which hinges on three factors. The first factor involves water movement. Turbulent water (as in a washing machine) makes it hard to establish an anchor since the water is already moving. To minimize this problem, find water that is not disturbed in front of you and stretch to reach it.

The second factor involves the pitch or angle of the hand(s). Recall that it is almost always best to put pressure on the water in a direction perpendicular to your direction of travel. As a general rule, your fingers should almost always be pointed slightly down on each stroke in order to encourage at least your hand to be perpendicular to your direction of travel.

The last factor is strength. If you do not yet have the strength to hold the water, your hand will waffle through it. Alternatively, being unable to hold the water may relate to bad balance, which can weaken the propulsive force enough that it does not overcome the drag force. Both of these issues can be corrected over time through practice.

Figure 2.2 **BASIC CATCH**

a

b

c

Preparation

1. Make sure you have a suitable space to perform the skill.
2. You can use a kickboard or pull buoy for the skill.

Execution

1. Place the kickboard under your chest for buoyancy and lay on the water facedown.
2. Once you have achieved a balanced position on the kickboard reach your arms forward above your head.
3. With the palms facing down, begin by pitching the fingers of the left hand down to make the palm of the hand perpendicular to the top of the water.
4. Pull the hand back toward the hip and thigh keeping, the hand perpendicular the whole way.
5. Return to the start position.
6. Try the same motion with the opposite arm.
7. For the breaststroke catch, begin in the start position with arms stretched out above the head and lying flat on the water with the kickboard still under your chest.
8. Sweep the hands out while simultaneously pitching the fingers down.
9. Pull back on the water until your hands are at a similar place to the top of the head on the top of the water.
10. Bring the elbows together as you move your hands back to the start position.
11. Repeat both catches a number of times.
12. These same execution steps can be performed with a pull buoy between the thighs in addition to the kickboard under the chest or instead of having the kickboard under the chest.

MISSTEP

You splash the water a lot.

CORRECTION

You can put effective pressure on the water only with your hands *in* the water. Avoid slapping the top of the water or pushing at the top.

MISSTEP

You push down with your palm toward the bottom of the pool.

CORRECTION

To provide propulsive force, get your hand (and as many other arm surfaces as possible) perpendicular to the direction in which you want to go.

DRILL FOR THE CATCH

The best way to develop kinesthetic awareness or feel for the water is to practice in-water drills that minimize other factors. The best drill for this is the dig.

Catch Drill   Dig

This three-part drill is best done in water in which you can stand. Using a stopwatch, measure how long it takes you to walk as fast as you can from one end of the pool to the other; record your time. Then repeat the walking exercise, but this time also use your hands to sweep water out of your way laterally, as if plowing the water one arm movement at a time. Once again, record your time. Next, use an overhand over-the-water motion to accomplish the same task and record your time. Which technique works best for you? (Simply walking should produce your slowest time.) Could you feel your hands anchoring in the water and pulling forward? You might repeat the drill a few times to ensure that you have done it correctly.

TO INCREASE DIFFICULTY

- Pull forcefully with your hands.
- Pull quickly with your hands.

TO DECREASE DIFFICULTY

- Walk at an easy pace, letting your hands provide balance.
- Use both arms at the same time.

Success Check

- You can make it down the pool faster when using the catch.
- You can alternate arms during the drill.

1 point: You can go faster than just walking, using the catch.

3 points: You can go faster than just walking and use both arms at the same time.

5 points: You can go much faster than just walking and alternate your arms.

SCULLING

The next skill in developing a feel for the water involves sculling (figure 2.3) and putting pressure on the water with both your hands and your forearms. Your hand position should be loose rather than rigid. Though some people advocate holding the hand like a paddle or spoon, a rigid hand position provides no meaningful hydro-dynamic advantage for most swimmers. The hand should be slightly curved like the blade of a propeller on a plane or boat. The curvature provides great ability to produce higher and lower areas of pressure similar to that also of an airplane wing.

Stand in the water with your back to the pool wall. Extend your arms straight out in front of you and sink to the point where your shoulders are just below the surface and your arms are completely covered with water. With your hands in a natural, relaxed position and slightly cupped, rotate your thumbs down so that your palms are angled slightly rather than parallel to the pool bottom.

Next, sweep your hands outward, making sure to keep your elbows straight. You should feel pressure from the water on your hands and forearms. Once your hands are about 2 feet (0.6 m) apart, rotate your thumbs up and your little fingers down so that, once again, your palms are slightly angled—only this time *toward* each other rather than away—and move your arms back to the original position. Again, keep your elbows straight.

Repeat this motion several times and adjust the pitch of your palms to get a good feel for the water. As you progress, angle your fingers down slightly as well. The sculling motion creates higher pressure on the palm side of your hand and lower pressure on the back of your hand, thus providing propulsive force.

Figure 2.3 SCULLING

a

b

Preparation

1. Check the water around you to ensure that you have enough room to perform the skill.
2. Make sure that you are in water no deeper than chest level.
3. Position yourself with plenty of distance to cover in the same depth of water.

Execution

1. Begin by lying on the water facedown.
2. Extend the arms in front and over your head.
3. With the hands slightly cupped, sweep the hands out and in with fingers pitching down toward the bottom of the pool.
4. Keeping the elbows and arms long but not locked, repeat the process until you can feel forward movement.

MISSTEP

You keep your hands very stiff.

CORRECTION

Relax your hands and feel the water.

MISSTEP

You don't go anywhere when sculling.

CORRECTION

Make sure that your hands are slightly cupped, which provides the same high-pressure and low-pressure propulsion as propellers and airplane wings. Water will flow faster over the top part of the hand as it has a greater distance to travel, and the inside arc of the hand has a smaller linear distance, so the water remains easier to hold. The faster moving water on the top of the hand is low pressure, and the palm would be higher pressure. To achieve equilibrium, the barrier (i.e., the hand) will move toward the lower pressure.

DRILL FOR SCULLING

Use the following drill to help practice the sculling skill.

Sculling Drill   Sculling With a Pull Buoy

Next, put this skill to work in a swimming position. Place a pull buoy between your legs slightly above your knees. Lie flat and facedown on the water in a neutral position, as described in step 1, with your arms extended above your head. Keep your hands relaxed, with your fingers pitched slightly downward, and slowly try the sculling motion until you feel yourself being pulled forward.

This is a complex skill that takes time to master. It requires movements that are not fast, rigid, or mechanical but slow, controlled, and fluid. Use slow, rhythmic movements and make sure that your hands never stop; they should be sweeping either out or in at any given time. Failure to master this skill does not prevent a person from swimming, but mastering it enables greater proficiency in later stages of the learning process. Repeat the drill several times, experimenting with hand angle and positioning to see what works best for you in creating propulsion. To develop a good catch, you must feel where the water pressure is on your hands and forearms!

TO INCREASE DIFFICULTY

- Do not use a pull buoy.

TO DECREASE DIFFICULTY

- Bend your elbows slightly.
- Use a swimmer's snorkel.

Success Check

- You can make it down the pool.
- You can move forward with just the sculling motion and your arms straight. The motion is back and forth with the hands slightly cupped.

Score Your Success

1 point: You can swim across half the pool.

3 points: You can go farther than half of the pool length with no snorkel.

5-7 points: You can make it all the way down the pool length with little difficulty.

KICKING

When done correctly, kicking is a powerful part of swimming. The first kick to master is the flutter kick (figure 2.4), which is part of both freestyle and backstroke swimming. It is performed with alternating leg movements designed to put pressure on the water via both up and down movements. The more surfaces you engage in applying pressure, the better. The basic idea here is to initiate the kick in the hip; it is also helpful to use the strong muscles of the core for propulsion, and that technique is addressed in future steps. For now, focus on the basics of kicking as a propulsive force.

The following drill progression helps you master the flutter kick. The first part of the progression helps you develop an effective mental image of what your legs are supposed to do. Of course, creatures evolved for swimming use well-adapted body parts to make movements that are long and fluid—for example, the movements of a fish, dolphin, or whale tail. Humans are at a disadvantage in this regard because we have solid bones in our legs rather than reticulated vertebrae, making us less flexible for fluid movement. In compensating for this deficit, it helps to envision the movement that you want. You might imagine, for instance, that the knee and ankle of each leg are connected by a rubber band. This image helps you keep your legs long and loose as you drive motion from your lower core.

Figure 2.4 FLUTTER KICKING

Preparation

1. Get in the water and grab the gutter.
2. From a standing position facing the wall, kick your legs up to the surface and make your body horizontal (parallel to the pool bottom).
3. At this stage, it is okay to use your forearms and the wall to help you achieve a horizontal position and to have your head out of the water.
4. Keep your legs as long and loose as possible (do not actively point your toes).

Execution

1. Make sure that you can sustain a steady rhythmic kick (speed is not important yet) that feels like you are putting pressure on the water all the way down the length of your leg (advanced swimmers have described this feeling as the water seeming to roll all the way down the leg and off the toes).
2. Once you are comfortable in the horizontal position, put your face in the water and extend your arms so that just your hands are on the wall.
3. As you continue to kick, you should feel your hands being pressed toward the wall. Maintain the same extended streamlined position that you developed in step 1. If your hands are grabbing the wall and hanging on instead of being pushed toward the wall, check yourself for correct positioning from hands to toes.

In earlier parts of step 2, you developed a mental image and achieved a horizontal position in the water while using your legs to maintain balance. The next part of this step ensures that the kick you are developing is propulsive. With proper kicking imagery, it is now time to use your legs to manipulate and put pressure on the water.

As your feet get to the surface, keep in mind that your goal is to put pressure on the water, which means that your legs must be *in* the water. Many novice swimmers equate kicking hard with big splashes; in reality, however, those splashes indicate that the energy exerted is being absorbed by the water rather than benefitting the swimmer. Try to have just your heel—rather than your whole foot—break the surface of the water. A quick head-to-toe check with the following questions in mind will help to make sure you are performing the skill correctly.

1. Are your arms extended all the way out?
2. Is your core long, or are you doing a "crunching" motion?
3. Is your pelvis tucked under rather than staying flat, thus causing your feet to sink?
4. Do you feel the effort in your glutes and upper thighs, which indicates that you are using your whole leg and core? Or do you feel it in your quads, near your knees, which indicates that you are using only your lower legs?
5. Are your ankles stiff or loose? Loose is good.

MISSTEP

You splash a lot.

CORRECTION

To achieve propulsive force, get your feet (and as much other leg surface as possible) in contact with the water. Keep your legs long and loose.

MISSTEP

You don't go anywhere when you kick.

CORRECTION

Rather than point your toes or make your leg stiff, imagine curling your toes. This approach keeps your feet flexed but prevents your legs from being stiff.

DRILLS FOR FLUTTER KICKING

Once you have gone through all of these helpful cues and can feel the pressure that you apply to the water, it is time to face the real test of propulsive force—kicking and actually providing some movement forward.

Kicking Drill 1   Fingertip Pressure

Move about a yard (m) away from the wall, then establish a neutral buoyant position on your front by lying on the water in the streamlined position described in step 1. Using only your kicking skill, kick toward the wall with your hands stretched out so that your fingertips touch the wall first. Once your fingers have touched the wall, continue kicking so that you feel pressure on your fingertips. This pressure indicates that you have developed a propulsive kick and can purposefully manipulate the water using your legs.

TO INCREASE DIFFICULTY

- Touch the wall with only a single finger.
- Exhale the whole time and repeat.

TO DECREASE DIFFICULTY

- Grab the gutter.
- Use a kickboard under your stomach to provide buoyancy.

Success Check

- You can stay at the wall.
- You can almost feel the water roll down your leg and off your toes.

Score Your Success

1 point: You can stay on the wall but need to use the gutter.

3 points: You can push your fingers into the wall but only for 5 or fewer seconds.

5–7 points: You can push your fingers into the wall for more than 10 seconds.

Kicking Drill 2   Kickboard

The next part of the progression ensures that your kick is indeed propulsive. Using a kickboard for balance only, place your hands on the lower corners of the board. Facing away from the wall in the water, pull your feet up, place them on the wall, and push off on your front. Make sure that your face is in the water and look directly at the bottom of the pool.

Now, begin the same rhythmic kicking that you developed earlier in this progression. It should propel you down the length of the pool at a very slow speed. If you come to a stop or even go backward, check for correct positioning from your hands to your toes. Many swimmers come to the pool with a limited range of motion in the ankles. Make sure that your ankles are slightly plantar-flexed, so that your toes point away from your body, but not so much as to make your legs rigid.

When you need to breathe, simply apply pressure to the kickboard and lift your head for air. Make this motion quick in order to maintain your balance in the water and get your face back in the water to stabilize your balance. As you progress in this part, try rotating the head to the side to breathe.

TO INCREASE DIFFICULTY

- Place your hands together on the kickboard.
- Use a less stable pull bouy in the place of a kickboard.
- Don't use a kickboard at all.

TO DECREASE DIFFICULTY

- Rest your forearms on the kickboard rather than merely grabbing the end of it.
- Use a swimmer's snorkel.

Success Check

- You can travel the length of the pool without any big splashes.
- You can turn your head to the side to breathe.

Score Your Success

1 point: You can go half of the pool length with your arms on the kickboard.

3 points: You can go half of the pool length with just your hands on the kickboard.

5–7 points: You can go the whole pool length with ease with just your hands.

KICKING WITHOUT A KICKBOARD

Once you have mastered the skill with the kickboard (using the Kickboard drill to practice), it is time once again to put your propulsive kicking force to the test. Repeat the process just described, but this time do it without the assistance of the kickboard (figure 2.5). The goal is to kick in a streamlined position. If you were able to do so with a kickboard, then this transition should be a little easier. The new challenge here is that when you breathe, you should use the same sculling motion described earlier in this step. Simply sweep your hands out and in rhythmically to apply enough pressure on the water to allow you to lift your head for a quick breath. You can then continue with a freestyle stroke. Once you have mastered this technique—and it may take a few tries—it is time to move to flutter kicking on your back.

Figure 2.5 FLUTTER KICKING WITHOUT A KICKBOARD

Preparation

1. Facing away from the wall in the water, pull your feet up, place them on the wall, and push off on your front.
2. Make sure that your face is in the water and look directly at the bottom of the pool.

Execution

1. Begin the same rhythmic kicking motion that you developed earlier in this progression; it should propel you down the length of the pool at a very slow speed.
2. Sweep your hands rhythmically out and in; apply enough pressure on the water to allow you to lift your head for a quick breath.

FLUTTER KICKING ON YOUR BACK

Flutter kicking on your back (figure 2.6) differs slightly from kicking on your front. Since you are on your back, the kicking motion is up for the most part (you will learn more about that later). Once again, it is helpful to develop an effective mental image—in this case, that of a soccer ball floating on the water that you kick up into the air with the top of your foot. This mental image helps you apply pressure in the right places and recruit the proper muscles. As with kicking on your front, imagine the joints of each leg being connected by a rubber band; staying long and loose is still a key.

Remember both your mental image and the feeling of pressure on the water from both the tops and the bottoms of your feet. Ensure that your toes just break the surface. As before, big splashes do not provide propulsive force and should be avoided. Kicking with your feet and legs coming out of the water makes big splashes. Since you are on your back, your toes will be the first to break the surface. As land-based creatures, we tend to have a natural affinity for leading this kick with the heel, as in a running or cycling motion. In correcting this tendency, it can be helpful to work with a kickboard (as described in the following Missteps section).

MISSTEP
You make big splashes while kicking with your heels first.

CORRECTION
Focus on the analogy of a whale or dolphin tail and try to replicate its long, fluid up-and-down motion.

Figure 2.6 FLUTTER KICKING ON YOUR BACK

a

b

c

Preparation

1. Lie on the water on your back with your hands at your sides for balance as described in step 1.

Execution

1. Keeping your legs long and loose, begin the flutter-kicking motion of alternating leg kicks. If necessary, you can hold onto the wall for support.

MISSTEP
Your knees keep breaking the water's surface.

CORRECTION
Hold a kickboard with both hands down at your hips, extending the kickboard over your knees. Now try the kicking motion again; if you feel your knees touching the board and making it bounce up and down, then you are not finishing your kick underwater and are probably leading with your heels or bicycling your kick.

DRILLS FOR KICKING WITHOUT A KICKBOARD

As you develop kicking proficiency, the following drills will help you to not rely on any equipment for balance or assistance.

Boardless Kicking Drill 1   Kicking on Your Back or Your Front

Once you have achieved propulsion in this position on the back, repeat this same part, the flutter kick on the back, but with your hands now above your head in a streamlined position. Doing so requires you to change your position on the water slightly—your spinal curvature will change—in order to compensate for not having your hands at your sides to help with balance. As before, you should feel the effort in your lower core, specifically there will be muscle contraction and fatigue in your upper thighs and glutes. If you have trouble achieving propulsion, do a simple hands-to-toes check for positioning and technique to ensure that you are doing it right. Once you have mastered this on your back, try the same on your front. When you go to breathe, rotate the head to the side as with the kickboard drill.

TO INCREASE DIFFICULTY

- Drop one arm.

TO DECREASE DIFFICULTY

- Have a friend or coach hold up your hands when you breathe.
- Use a swimmer's snorkel.

Success Check

- You can travel down the length of the pool without any big splashes.
- You can turn your head to the side to breathe.

Score Your Success

1 point: You can go half of the pool length with assistance.

3 points: You can go half of the pool length with no assistance.

5–7 points: You can go the whole pool length with ease and without assistance.

Boardless Kicking Drill 2   Underwater Kicking

Once you have mastered flutter kicking on both your back and your front on the surface of the water, it is time to fine-tune your kick for maximum benefit. In previous parts of this progression, you have learned how to apply pressure to the water with your legs, feet, and toes. The instructions have emphasized kicking in a specific direction, but the most effective and efficient swimmers can manipulate the water by applying pressure with both the tops and the bottoms of their legs and feet.

The next part of developing this ability involves kicking on a streamline under the water. Remember that at no point should you engage in extended breath holding! Remember also to exhale slowly.

As described in step 1, put both feet on the wall and assume a position in which your head, knees, and toes are up. Release the hand from the wall, touch your hands together under the water, and push off in a streamlined position while keeping your head down. Kick underwater for as long as you can before needing a breath; keep your legs long and loose and kick both up and down. Repeat this skill several times; it can be difficult to find your balance while putting pressure on the water, but you will master the skill with enough repetition.

TO INCREASE DIFFICULTY

- Increase the number of kicks off the wall.

TO DECREASE DIFFICULTY

- Use fins.

Success Check	*Score Your Success*
• You can travel down the length of the pool without surfacing.	1 point: You can go 10 yards underwater.
• You can feel the pressure from the water on both the tops and the bottoms of your feet.	3 points: You can go more than 15 yards underwater.

DOLPHIN KICK

The next propulsive motion to learn is that of the dolphin, or butterfly, kick. Though somewhat similar to the flutter kick, this technique for manipulating the water is a little more difficult to master. Instead of alternating the legs, this kick keeps the legs together as if they were bonded, thus mimicking closely the motion of a dolphin's tale. The advantage of this kick is that it applies more surface area to the water to produce more propulsive force.

Dolphin Kicking at the Wall

Unlike the flutter kick, this kick (figure 2.7) derives its power from the middle part of the core—from the lower part of the rib cage down through the pelvis. Let the strong muscles of your core initiate most of the work. Your legs should stay together the entire time, and, as with the flutter kick, they should be long and loose. A good mental image for this kick is the motion of a dolphin or whale; try to mimic that motion with your body, from your chest on down. Some swimmers also find it helpful to imagine that their legs are glued together and cannot be separated. To work on this skill, use the same progression used for the flutter kick on your front.

Figure 2.7   DOLPHIN KICKING AT THE WALL

Preparation

1. Get in the water and grab the gutter.
2. From a standing position facing the wall, kick your legs up to the surface and make your body horizontal and parallel to the pool bottom.
3. Use your forearms and the wall to help you achieve a horizontal position and keep your head out of the water.
4. Put your face into the water and extend your arms so that only your hands are on the wall.

Execution

1. Drive your hips back and forth by using the strong muscles of your core; use your legs merely to finish off the kick.
2. As you continue to kick, you should feel your hands being pressed toward the wall.

In the first few parts of this progression, you have developed a mental image and achieved a horizontal position in the water using your legs to maintain your balance. The next part is to make sure that the kick you are developing is propulsive. You should be in the same extended streamlined position that you developed in step 1. If your hands are grabbing the wall and hanging on instead of being pushed toward it, do a simple hands-to-toes check for proper positioning.

Dolphin Kicking Away From the Wall

Once you have gone through these helpful cues and can feel the pressure you are applying to the water, it is time for the real test of propulsive force, butterfly kicking away from the wall (figure 2.8).

Figure 2.8 **DOLPHIN KICKING AWAY FROM THE WALL**

Preparation

1. Move about a yard (m) away from the wall, then establish a neutral buoyant position on your front by lying on the water in the streamlined position as described in step 1.

Execution

1. Using only your kicking skill, kick toward the wall with your hands stretched out so that your fingertips touch the wall first.

2. Once your fingers have touched the wall, continue kicking so that you feel pressure on your fingertips. This pressure indicates that you have developed a propulsive kick and can manipulate the water using your legs.

MISSTEP

You just wiggle in the water.

CORRECTION

The kick starts at the rib cage and works its way down, much like the motion of a jump rope that has been flipped. Keep your lower legs loose.

MISSTEP

You nod up and down to make yourself go.

CORRECTION

The kick comes from the lower core and rib cage; try not to move as if you were bobbing for apples.

MISSTEP

Your hands are grabbing on to the wall.

CORRECTION

Extend the arms and make sure your kick is propulsive rather than having the arms do the work of holding you to the wall.

MISSTEP

You curl up and push at the water with your feet.

CORRECTION

Keep the legs long and loose. Rather than pointing the toes, think about curling them as if picking a penny up off the pool deck.

Dolphin Kicking on Your Back

Dolphin kicking on your back (figure 2.9) differs only slightly from kicking on your front. As before, developing an appropriate mental image for the action can help you apply pressure in the right places and recruit the proper muscles. The mental image here, as with kicking on your front, is to think of your leg joints as being connected by a rubber band; staying long and loose is still a key.

MISSTEP

The water washes back up to your face.

CORRECTION

The two most likely culprits are your knees breaking the surface of the water and the tops of your feet "pushing" at the water. To correct this misstep and produce a propulsive kick, hold a kickboard with your hands down at your hips, extending the kickboard over your knees. Now try the kicking motion again; if you feel your knees touching the board and making it bounce up and down, you are not finishing you kick underwater and are probably leading with your heels or bicycling your kick.

Figure 2.9 **DOLPHIN KICKING ON YOUR BACK**

Preparation

1. Lie on the water on your back with your hands at your sides to help with balance as described in step 1. Or, if necessary, you can hold on to the wall for support. Keeping your legs long and loose, begin the dolphin kicking motion.

Execution

1. Drive your hips back and forth by using the strong muscles of your core; use your legs merely to finish off the kick.

DRILLS FOR DOLPHIN KICKING

As you perform these drills, keep your legs as long and loose as possible (do not actively point your toes). As your feet get to the surface, keep in mind that your goal is to put pressure on the water, which means that your legs must be *in* the water. The keys here are to sustain a steady rhythmic kick (do not worry about being fast just yet) that feels like you are putting pressure on the water all the way down your leg. Once you have mastered this skill, it is time to move on to the next part of the progression.

Dolphin Kick Drill 1   Kickboard

The next part of the progression is to ensure that your kick is indeed propulsive. In the water, use a kickboard for balance only, placing your hands on the lower corners of the board. Facing away from the wall, pull your feet up, place them on the wall, and push off on your front. Make sure that your face is in the water and look directly at the bottom of the pool.

Now begin the same rhythmic kicking motion that you developed earlier in this progression. It should propel you down the length of the pool at a very slow speed. If you come to a stop or even go backward, check for correct positioning from your hands to your toes. Many swimmers come to the pool with a limited range of motion in the ankles. Make sure that your ankles are slightly plantar-flexed, so that your toes point away from your body but not so much as to make your legs rigid.

When you need to breathe, simply apply pressure to the kickboard and lift your head for air. Make this motion quick in order to maintain your balance in the water and get your face back in the water to stabilize your balance.

TO INCREASE DIFFICULTY

- Place one hand on the kickboard and kick on your side (right side for 25 kicks and left side for 25 kicks).
- Eliminate the kickboard and kick in a streamlined position.
- Kick underwater in a streamlined position.

TO DECREASE DIFFICULTY

- Use fins to prevent that stalling feeling and avoid rushing the drill.
- Lay your upper arms across the kickboard by gripping the top of the board to keep your face out of the water. Be aware that doing so may put extra stress on your lower back.
- Use a swimmer's snorkel.

Success Check

- You can perform the drill while maintaining a long body line.
- You are not breaking the surface or too deep after the first pullout.

Score Your Success

1 point: You can go somewhere but need to lie on the kickboard.

2 points: The kickboard is extended, but you need fins.

3 points: You can do very well with the kickboard extended and no fins.

4 points: You can go without the board but need fins.

5–7 points: You are an expert, needing neither board nor fins.

Dolphin Kick Drill 2   Without a Kickboard

Once you have mastered the skill with the kickboard, it is time once again to put your propulsive kicking force to the test. Repeat the process just described, but this time do it without the assistance of the kickboard. The goal is to kick in a streamlined position. If you were able to do so with a kickboard, then this transition should be a little easier. The new challenge here is that when you breathe, you should use the same sculling motion described earlier in this step. Simply sweep your hands out and in rhythmically to apply enough pressure on the water to allow you time to lift your head for a quick breath. Once you have mastered this technique—and it may take a few tries—it is time to move to dolphin kicking on your back.

TO INCREASE DIFFICULTY

- Place one hand on the kickboard and kick on your side (right side for 25 kicks and left side for 25 kicks).
- Eliminate the kickboard and kick in a streamlined position.
- Kick underwater in a streamlined position.

TO DECREASE DIFFICULTY

- Use fins to prevent that stalling feeling and avoid rushing the drill.
- Rest your upper arms across the kickboard by gripping the top to keep your face out of the water. Be aware that doing so may put extra stress on your lower back.
- Use a swimmer's snorkel.

Success Check

- You can perform the drill while maintaining a long body line.
- You are not breaking the surface or too deep after the first pullout.

Score Your Success

1 point: You can go somewhere but need to lie on the kickboard.

2 points: The kickboard is extended, but you need fins.

3 points: You can do very well with the kickboard extended and no fins.

4 points: You can go without the board but need fins.

5–7 points: You are an expert, needing neither fins nor board.

Dolphin Kick Drill 3   On Your Back

This drill is essentially the same as kicking on your front but without the kickboard. It is best to do it in a streamlined position if you can. The purpose of this drill is to help you develop the ability to put pressure on the water in an up-and-down fashion.

TO INCREASE DIFFICULTY

- Kick underwater in a streamlined position. Propulsive force can be generated with an asymmetrical kick; however, maximum propulsion comes from kicking in both directions. This capability comes into play in both the butterfly and the backstroke.

TO DECREASE DIFFICULTY

- Use fins to prevent that stalling feeling and avoid rushing the drill.
- Rest your upper arms across the kickboard by gripping the top to keep your face out of the water. Be aware that doing so may put extra stress on your lower back.
- Use a swimmer's snorkel.

Success Check

- You can maintain a long body line and perform the drill.
- You are not breaking the surface or too deep after the first pullout.

Score Your Success

1 point: You can go somewhere but need to lie on the kickboard.

2 points: The kickboard is extended, but you need fins.

3 points: You can do very well with the kickboard extended and no fins.

4 points: You can go without the board but need fins.

5–7 points: You are an expert, needing neither fins nor board.

BREASTSTROKE KICK

The last kicking skill is the breaststroke kick (figure 2.10). Draw your heels up to your hips while keeping your knees close together, then point your toes out and apply pressure to the water with your insteps and the inside calf of each leg. The kick is performed simultaneously with both legs. The following progression helps you ensure that you are doing it correctly to provide maximum propulsion.

Figure 2.10 BREASTSTROKE KICK WITH ONE LEG

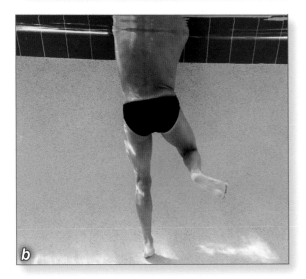

Preparation

1. Begin by standing near the pool wall in water that is at least chest deep. Be sure that your chest is touching the wall.

2. Starting with your right leg, draw your heel up with your knee still touching the wall in the dorsiflexed or L position. Once your thigh is parallel to the bottom of the pool, stop raising the leg.

Execution

1. While in this position, slide your heel out and away from the centerline of your body while keeping your knee in the same place. This action may seem awkward at first. The key is to make sure that your heel is farther from the center of your body than your knee is. You may need to use the wall for balance.

2. Once your foot is in position, push the instep in a sweeping motion down toward the bottom of the pool. You have succeeded when you can feel pressure from the water on your instep and on the inside of your calf.

3. Once you have succeeded with your right foot, try the same motion with your left foot.

Breaststroke Kick With Both Legs

If you can feel pressure in the critical areas when breaststroke-kicking with each leg, then you are ready to try both legs together (figure 2.11). Some swimmers have problems with flexibility in the hips, knees, and ankles and are not as effective as others, so do not let this frustrate you. For most people, this action requires several repetitions to master.

Figure 2.11 **BREASTSTROKE KICK WITH BOTH LEGS**

a

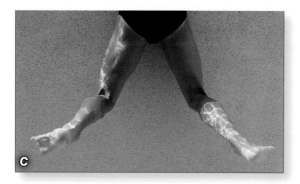

b

c

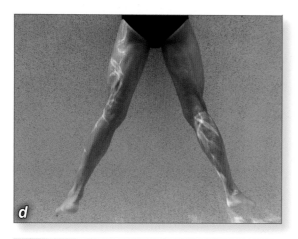

d

Preparation

1. Find deeper water and anchor your arms with your hands or elbows to the gutter or deck so that your legs hang free.

Execution

1. Using the same motion described for breaststroke kick with one leg, draw up both heels. Next, push both heels out while keeping your knees close together, then sweep your feet together in a circular motion.

2. Your heels should be wider apart than your knees; ideally, your knees should be no more than hip-width apart when your heels are outside of your knees.

3. You should feel some lift from your insteps and the inside of your calves putting pressure on the water.

Breaststroke Kick With Propulsion

Now that you feel the pressure on the water, it is time to ensure that it is propulsive pressure by moving through the water (figure 2.12). The next part of the progression involves lying on your back in the neutral position described in step 1 with your hands at your sides for balance. Once you have achieved equilibrium, draw your heels up while trying to keep your upper legs underwater. This is slightly different from being on the wall but involves the same type of movement.

Once your heels are close to your hips, rotate your heels out so that they are wider than your knees, then sweep them together. As before, this motion is more about pressure on the water than about the speed of the movement. Squeeze your ankles together. Did you move? The pressure on the water should have caused you to move headfirst. Once you have completed one kick, return to the neutral position and let your momentum fade. Repeat the same motion until you are comfortable with it.

Figure 2.12 **BREASTSTROKE KICK WITH PROPULSION**

Preparation

1. Perform the wall exercise for the breaststroke kick with both legs first.
2. Once you feel the pressure on your insteps and calves, you are ready to move to the lane.
3. Make sure that there is plenty of room to perform the skill, then find your back-floating position as described in step 1.

Execution

1. With your arms fully extended, elbows locked, and hands on the end of the kickboard, push off of the wall.
2. Draw your heels up as you did when practicing on the wall.
3. Push your heels out and point your toes toward the opposite side of the pool.
4. Sweep your heels together to finish the kick.
5. As your heels come together, point your toes back and glide.
6. Stop before hitting your head on the pool wall; as you may remember, the backstroke flags in competition pools are located 5 yards from the wall.

MISSTEP

You lead with your knees, which come out of the water first.

CORRECTION

Keep your knees together and sweep out with your heels, sweeping lower legs together. Keep your lower legs loose.

MISSTEP

You keep your toes pointed.

CORRECTION

The kick depends on grabbing the water with your insteps; change the flexion of your ankles so that you feel it there.

Breaststroke Kick Drill   Kickboard

The next part of the progression is to transfer this skill to the front. Using a kickboard, repeat the same motions that you performed on your back. The key is to make your movements slow and correct. Once you feel comfortable on your front with the kickboard, put the board away and try the skill in the streamlined position. When you need to breathe, use the same sculling motion described earlier; remember to breathe out slowly.

TO INCREASE DIFFICULTY

* Stay in a streamlined position.
* Place a pull buoy between your legs slightly above your mid-thighs to ensure that your knees stay together.

TO DECREASE DIFFICULTY

* Use a kickboard in front or even lie on it.
* Use a swimmer's snorkel.

Success Check

* You can push with an effective kick with both legs while keeping your knees no more than 12 inches (30 cm) apart.
* You can go 25 yards with ease on your front.

Score Your Success

1 point: You can go 10 yards with correct form.

3 points: You can go 25 yards with correct form.

5 points: You can go 25 yards in more than 15 kicks.

7 points: You can go 25 yards in 15 or fewer kicks.

SUCCESS SUMMARY

In step 2, you have learned a bit about drag force and propulsive force. In future steps, you will learn to produce fast and efficient strokes, but as of now you have already mastered some basic kicking skills that will help you along the path to becoming a better swimmer. Specifically, you should have mastered the following skills:

1. Achieving an aquatic position that minimizes drag
2. Feeling the water and where it slips off of your hands when anchoring your hands during the catch phase
3. Using a sculling motion to provide propulsion
4. Using flutter, dolphin, and breaststroke kicks to provide propulsion, both on your back and on your front

SCORE YOUR SUCCESS

If you scored 45 to 49 points, then you have passed this step; even so, you might go back and revisit any skills in which you scored poorly. If you scored 50 to 60 points, then you did a very good job on this step and are comfortable in the water. If you scored more than 60 points, then you did exceptionally well.

Catch Drills

1. Dig   ___ out of 5
2. Sculling With a Pull Buoy   ___ out of 7

Flutter-Kick Drills

1. Fingertip Pressure   ___ out of 7
2. Kickboard   ___ out of 7

Boardless Kicking Drills

1. Kicking on Your Back or Your Front   ___ out of 7
2. Underwater Kicking   ___ out of 3

Dolphin Kick Drills

1. Kickboard   ___ out of 7
2. Without a Kickboard   ___ out of 7
3. On Your Back   ___ out of 7

Breaststroke Kick Drill

1. Kickboard   ___ out of 7
   Total   ___ **out of 64**

Freestyle

Over the years, versions of freestyle swimming have gone by many names, including trudgen stroke, Australian crawl, and front crawl. Competitive freestyle was born in the late 1800s, when John Arthur Trudgen witnessed native South Americans swimming with an overhand recovery and a wide, scissorlike kick. He carried the stroke back to England, where it took on his name despite being characterized as un-European barbaric thrashing.

Around the turn of the century in Australia, a similar stroke was used with a flutter kick by a Solomon Islander named Alick Wickham. That version was developed further by coach Richmond "Dick" Cavill into what we now recognize as something closer to freestyle, which was referred to as the Australian crawl. In the modern era, coaches added a six-beat (i.e., six kicks per one arm stroke) kick, and the stroke became the front crawl, which later came to be referred to simply as freestyle. Technically speaking, freestyle races can be swum using any stroke, but the crawl stroke is the fastest of the competitive strokes and therefore has become synonymous with freestyle.

THE THREE Rs

Good freestyle depends on the three Rs: reach, rotation, and relaxation. Reach is discussed with the catch and pull. Rotation involves turning the body over by rotating around the anchor point—the hand. It is crucial to ensure that your hip and shoulder stay in the same plane. Relaxation involves learning to relax the body parts that are not helping you swim more efficiently.

Good freestyle is efficient and effective. Swimmers who master freestyle find it is as easy as walking. To that end, this step helps you develop the following skills:

- Horizontal body line
- Rotation on a long axis
- High elbow catch
- Pressure on the water throughout the stroke
- Kicking rhythm
- Effective breathing
- Effective timing

Once you have mastered all of these skills, you are well on your way to an effective freestyle stroke.

One key element of effective freestyle is maintaining a good horizontal position on the water. As mastered in step 1 (specifically, floating on your front), the basic position involves lying on the water with your head, hips, feet, and hands all at the surface of the water. As you remain stretched out on the water, ensure that your face is in the water and that you are looking straight down at the bottom of the pool.

BASIC FREESTYLE STROKE

A good freestyle armstroke consists of four basic elements that provide the bulk of the propulsive force for swimming: catch, pull, finish, and recovery. The first is the catch. Beginning with the left hand, you will want to pitch the fingers down so that the hand is perpendicular to the direction you want to go (figure 3.1*a*). As the hand pitches down, you will rotate the elbow and shoulder so that the forearm is also perpendicular to the direction you want to go. The second element is the pull. During this part of the stroke, you will pull the arm through so that the hand and forearm stay perpendicular to the direction you are going and the elbow remains bent (figure 3.1*b*). The finish of the stroke is next (figure 3.1*c*). As you progress through the middle and your arm is about midway down your body, you will transition from a pulling motion to that of a pushing motion almost as if you were going to try to slap your thigh with your hand. Lastly is the recovery (figure 3.1*d*). At this point you will raise the arm out of the water almost as if pulling your hand out of your pocket and bring it back to the front position where you started by sliding your hand fingers first into the water 8 to 10 inches above your head and extending the arm fully after that. Repeat this same motion with your right arm and hand and then stop. Remember that as you work on mastering a skill, it is crucial to move in a slow and controlled manner at first. As you may notice, kicking is not mentioned here; this does not mean that you should not kick but simply that you should focus on the skill being described.

Figure 3.1 BASIC FREESTYLE STROKE

Preparation

1. Beginning with your right hand, pitch your fingers down so that your hand is perpendicular to the direction in which you want to go.

2. As you pitch your hand down, rotate your elbow and shoulder so that your forearm is also perpendicular to the direction in which you want to go.

Execution

1. Pull your arm through so that your hand and forearm

remain perpendicular to the direction in which you are going and your elbow remains bent.

2. As you progress through the middle—and once your arm is about midway down your body—transition from a pulling motion to a pushing motion, almost as if you were trying to slap your thigh with your hand.

Follow-Through

1. Raise your arm out of the water, almost as if pulling your hand out of your pocket. Next, bring it back to the front position, where you started, by sliding your hand fingers-first into the water about 8 to 10 inches (20-25 cm) above your head and then extending your arm fully.

MISSTEP
Your feet sink.

CORRECTION
Use a pull buoy between your thighs to help with balance. You will not need this aid once you develop a good kick.

MISSTEP

You push your hand straight down toward the bottom of the pool and your head comes out of the water as you make a big circle with your arm.

CORRECTION

Think of the motion as reaching for something on a high shelf or reaching over a barrel. This image helps you remember to pitch your fingers down and rotate your elbow up to get an early vertical forearm.

MISSTEP

You pull your hand out at your hip and rush to get back to the front.

CORRECTION

Think of trying to slap your thigh with your hand. Since water cannot be compressed, you won't be able to do it, but the image helps you remember to finish the stroke.

FREESTYLE STROKE CYCLE

Once you have gone through one stroke cycle—one right arm and one left arm—it is time to put together multiple stroke cycles (figure 3.2). Remember that (unlike in some other sports) faster is not always better in swimming. Keep your movements slow and deliberate. The real objective in this part of your development is to anchor your hand and forearm in the water and pull yourself over them. Stop when you need air.

Figure 3.2 **FREESTYLE STROKE CYCLE**

Preparation

1. Start near the wall. As in step 1, push off in a streamlined position with your face in the water.

Execution

1. Begin with whichever arm is most comfortable for you and take as many strokes as you can on one breath while exhaling slowly.

2. Repeat this process several times, trying to get farther down the pool with the same number of strokes.

MISSTEP

You make a lot of splashing and thrashing movements.

CORRECTION

Splashing and thrashing indicate that the water is absorbing your energy and thus becoming turbulent. Turbulence makes it difficult to put pressure on the water. To correct this misstep, think about slipping your hand into a glove during the recovery (reentry into the water) and slapping your thigh at the end of the stroke. It is best to use long, controlled movements.

MISSTEP

You cannot get your arm fully out of the water on the recovery.

CORRECTION

As you finish the stroke, rotate your hip on the same side as the stroking arm and the shoulder of your stroking arm toward the sky. This action allows your upper arm to be more vertical without reaching behind your back, which is not an easy position to attain and expends considerable energy.

Armstroke Drill 3   Hands in Fists

This is a classic drill used to promote an early vertical forearm for an effective catch and pull. Instead of using an open hand for propulsion and holding the water, make a fist with each hand. There will be some splashing on the entry, but this drill compels you to get your elbow up and pull with the surface area of your forearm.

TO INCREASE DIFFICULTY

- Hold a tennis ball or racquetball in each hand to further decrease the surface area of your hands.
- Wrap your fingers over the end of a paddle (one in each hand) without using the straps. The minute your elbow drops, the paddle pulls away from your arm, thus making it harder to hold the paddle.

TO DECREASE DIFFICULTY

- Use fins to prevent that stalling feeling and isolate the catch and pull.
- Use a pull buoy to maintain balance.
- Use a swimmer's snorkel.

Success Check

- You can perform the drill while maintaining a long body line.
- You keep each hand closed in a tight fist.
- You swim reasonably well by just pulling with your forearm.

Score Your Success

1 point: You can do the drill but beat on the water (splashing).

2 points: You can do the pull drill correctly with fins or a pull buoy.

3 points: You can do the drill correctly but only for a few strokes.

4 points: You can do the drill correctly for 25 yards with a swimmer's snorkel.

5–10 points: You can do the drill correctly for at least 25 yards (5 points) and perhaps up to 50 yards (10 points). 1 point for each additional 10 yards.

ROTATION

To perform an effective recovery, you must be able to use your core muscles to turn your hip and shoulder over as one piece (figure 3.3). This skill also helps you develop an effective catch and pull, which in freestyle swimming means that you can reach farther. In addition, effective rotation helps set up a good position in which to get air. Try this exercise on the pool deck.

Figure 3.3 **ROTATION**

Preparation

1. Make sure the lane is clear, and there is at least 25 yards of space to perform the skill.
2. Push off the wall and steamline.

Execution

1. Begin swimming freestyle.
2. As you swim, pay special attention to where your upper arm is in relation to the water.
3. The closer to vertical the upper arm is, the better the rotation in the upper torso is.
4. Let the hips rotate with the shoulder as one piece.

DRILLS FOR ROTATION

Rotation through the core has been the subject of much recent debate in competitive swimming. Some competitors swim flatter, with little rotation, whereas others swim through the hips with considerable rotation. Both approaches can be correct, depending on the swimmer, but the most sustainable recreational swimming allows for most people to use the core to aid in rotation rather than relying on spinal flexibility. Some swimmers have more flexibility and strength in the spine and torso, allowing them to twist easier.

Rotation Drill 1   Tap Your Head

This drill gives you feedback about where your hands are in relation to the centerline of your body and your axis of rotation, as well as the vertical position of your head. It also compels you to rotate your body to perform the drill correctly. With all that said, the drill itself is very simple. Gently touch your fingertips to the crown of your head on the recovery, then place your hand in the water to recover for the next catch and pull. As in the catch-up drill, wait until one hand has completely recovered before beginning the next catch.

TO INCREASE DIFFICULTY

- Perform six kicks per stroke.

TO DECREASE DIFFICULTY

- Use fins to prevent that stalling feeling and avoid rushing the drill.
- Use a pull buoy to maintain balance.
- Use a swimmer's snorkel.

Success Check

- You can perform the drill while maintaining a long body line.
- You recover your hand slowly and just tap the crown of your head with your fingertips.
- There is little or no splash on entry.
- Your hands don't cross in front of your head (i.e., don't go past your centerline).

Score Your Success

1 point: You can tap your head, but the tap is more like a smack, and you need fins or a pull buoy.

2 points: You can do the pull drill correctly but need fins or a pull buoy.

3 points: You can do the drill correctly for a few strokes.

4 points: You can do the drill correctly for 25 yards with a swimmer's snorkel.

5–10 points: You can do the drill correctly for at least 25 yards (5 points) and perhaps up to 50 yards (10 points). 1 point per each addition 5 yards.

Rotation Drill 2   **Pull Buoy Between the Ankles**

This is a great drill for isolating your core (rather than your kick) as the primary cause of rotation. Place a pull buoy between your ankles and swim as usual in a slow, controlled fashion. Swimmers who swim "flat" rather than rotating will find their feet fishtailing all over the pool. To avoid or correct this problem, concentrate on using your core muscles to rotate your body and try to get your upper arm (from shoulder to elbow) as close to vertical as possible.

TO INCREASE DIFFICULTY

- Close your eyes and complete 10 arms strokes in a 25-yard pool while concentrating only on arm position.

TO DECREASE DIFFICULTY

- Use a swimmer's snorkel.

Success Check

- You can perform the drill while maintaining a long body line.
- You can avoid fishtailing or wiggling down the lane.

Score Your Success

1 point: You can rotate, but your hips and feet snake through the water.

3 points: You can do the drill correctly for a few strokes.

4 points: You can do the drill correctly for 25 yards with a swimmer's snorkel.

5–10 points: You can do the drill correctly for at least 25 yards (5 points) and perhaps up to 50 yards (10 points). 1 point for each additional 10 yards.

Rotation Drill 3   **20-20**

The 20-20 drill is simple to perform and helps you concentrate on both your rotation and the efficiency of your catching and pulling. The first part of the drill involves seeing how far you can go in 20 strokes. Repeat this part multiple times, trying to better your distance each time. The second part of drill involves seeing how far you can go in 20 breaths; this is discussed in the next section and helps you become more efficient.

TO INCREASE DIFFICULTY

- Perform six kicks per stroke.

TO DECREASE DIFFICULTY

- Use a pull buoy to maintain balance.
- Use a swimmer's snorkel.

(continued)

Rotation Drill 3 *(continued)*

Success Check

- You can do 20 strokes slowly and efficiently.
- You can go at least 25 yards with 20 strokes.
- You can swim easily without breathing on every stroke.

1 point: You can do 20 strokes, traveling less than 25 yards.

3 points: You can do 20 strokes and travel more than 25 yards.

4 points: You can do 20 strokes and travel more than 30 yards.

5–10 points: You can do 20 strokes and travel more than 40 yards.

BREATHING

As land-based creatures, we cannot process oxygen out of water as fish do; therefore, we must find a way to breathe air while swimming. In freestyle, this need is met by rotating the head so that the mouth and nose are out of the water at a good time during the stroke cycle (figure 3.4), thus allowing the swimmer to breathe without interrupting his or her rhythm. The best way to do so is to rotate the face out of the water as an arm is finishing a stroke at the thigh and beginning the recovery. The rotation is initiated at the shoulder and hip, and the head follows.

This technique is less about rotating the neck and more about proper positioning. There is a bow wave with the forward propulsion that allows for a trough to be produced; the depth and utility of that differ from swimmer to swimmer. A bow wave in the world of fluid mechanics is a wave that is produced by the vector displacement of water by another object. The size of the crest and trough produced depends on the mass, velocity, and displacement buoyancy of the object. As the body moves through the water, the crown of the head will cause the water in front of it to increase in pressure as the head moves forward. The water will seek equilibrium from this high pressure state by moving to a lower pressure. Due to the incompressibility of water, the water molecules "choose" a direction to go with some moving down and others moving up or to the side with and infinite number of vector possibilities. The rising part is offset by a falling part producing both a crest and a trough which is below the waterline and will be helpful when trying to rotate the mouth and nose toward the air to breathe. The objective here is to get your air as quickly as possible so that you can get your face back in the water before your hand finishes the recovery, thus readying you for the next catch.

Figure 3.4 **SINGLE-STROKE BREATHING**

Preparation

1. As you did in working on the basic armstroke, push off of the wall and begin your armstrokes.

Execution

1. While stroking with your arms, slowly exhale until you have expelled much of the air from your lungs.

2. As you finish your next stroke, rotate your body and face so that your face is out of the water, then breathe in and stop.

At this point, you should be on your side or back with one arm at your side and the other arm above your head, in front of your shoulder. Practice this sequence several times. Most people prefer one side or the other for rotation, so multiple repeats are helpful to identify which side is preferred. Then move on to continuous breathing (figure 3.5).

Figure 3.5 **CONTINUOUS BREATHING**

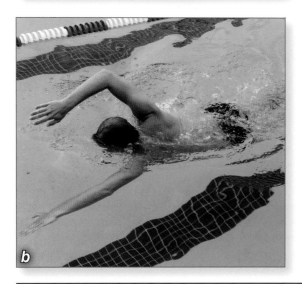

Preparation

1. Follow the steps for single-stroke breathing in figure 3.4.

Execution

1. Rotate your face back into the water and continue swimming. Rotate your face out of the water with a special emphasis on rotating the chin out.
2. Once you have mastered rotation to the side and gotten a quick breath, rotate your face back in while your hand recovers, then repeat the process.
3. Remember that slower movements are better at this point.

MISSTEP
You swallow water when trying to breathe.

CORRECTION
Are you lifting your head to vertical and looking forward instead of rotating? Doing so brings your mouth and nose closer to the surface of the water; instead, think about rotating your chin out while leaving one eye in the water.

MISSTEP
Your hips sink when you go to breathe.

CORRECTION
Make sure that you are looking to the side of the pool rather than lifting your head to look forward.

DRILLS FOR BREATHING

Breathing is more about timing than about anything else. Swimming is one of only a few sports in which your breathing is a life-and-death decision. When running or participating in other sports, your respiration is not really something you have to consciously think about when participating. Swimming on the other had is different. Inhaling with your face in the water will produce some unwanted consequences, including death. This factor is particularly important for new swimmers. As you progress through the skills, you may find yourself holding your breath, which is a mistake. Make sure to exhale slowly and inhale rhythmically rather than gulping at the air.

Breathing Drill 1   One-Arm

The one-arm freestyle drill comes in several versions. One of the most effective approaches is to stroke with only one arm down the length of the pool with the other arm at your side. On every stroke, breathe to the nonstroking side and be sure to rotate to the stroking side. The timing of this drill is crucial. It must be done slowly, and the shoulder of the stroking arm should be touching your ear when you breathe. In addition, your stroking arm should be fully extended until your face is back in the water to initiate the catch. Repeat the process by switching arms.

Breathing on both sides is a great skill to master, but many swimmers prefer one side or the other. Forty years ago, coaches advocated that one needed to learn to breathe on both sides in order to be a good swimmer. Enter Grant Hackett, multiple world-record holder and Olympic champion, who breathed exclusively on the right side. Michael Phelps, the most decorated Olympian in history, does the same thing. In addition, forcing the issue of breathing on both sides detracts from the needed focus on your propulsive movements. The breathing question can be addressed (if at all) once you progress far enough to work with a swim coach.

TO INCREASE DIFFICULTY

- Perform six kicks per stroke.

TO DECREASE DIFFICULTY

- Use fins to prevent that stalling feeling and isolate the catch and pull, as well as the timing of your breathing. Make sure that your face is back in the water before you initiate the catch.

Success Check

- You can perform the drill while maintaining a long body line.
- You rotate to both sides.
- You can breathe to your nonstroking side on every stroke.

Score Your Success

1 point: You can do the drill with fins.

2 points: You can do the pull drill but need fins, and your hand starts the stroke before your face is back in the water.

3 points: You can do the drill correctly for a few strokes.

4 points: You can do the drill correctly for 25 yards to one side.

5–10 points: You can do the drill correctly to each side for at least 25 yards (5 points) and perhaps up to 50 yards (10 points). 1 point per additional 5 yards.

Breathing Drill 2   3-5-3-7

This is a popular drill used to train breath control and relaxation. It is *not* designed to have swimmers hold their breath. The numbers (3, 5, 3, 7) indicate how many strokes you should take between breaths per 25 yards. In other words, for the first 25 yards, breathe every three strokes; for the second 25, breathe every five strokes, and so on. This drill is challenging even when done slowly and with effective movements, and the odd numbers cause an alternating of the breathing pattern. This alternating pattern is a great skill to have, especially for racers, triathletes, and open-water swimmers. It helps with having a faster breathing rate at higher workload levels, and it can aid in navigation for open-water swimmers.

TO INCREASE DIFFICULTY

• Change the breathing pattern every 50 yards instead of every 25.

TO DECREASE DIFFICULTY

• Use fins to prevent that stalling feeling and isolate the catch and pull.
• Use a pull buoy to maintain balance.

Success Check

• You can perform the breathing pattern.
• You can breathe on both sides easily.

Score Your Success

1 point: You can do the pull drill, making 3 and 5 of the sequence only with fins or a pull buoy.

2 points: You can do the drill with fins or a pull buoy.

3 points: You can do the drill correctly for at least 75 yards.

5–10 points: You can do the drill correctly for at least 100 yards (5 points) and perhaps up to 200 yards (10 points). 1 point for each additional 10 yards.

Breathing Drill 3   20-20 With Breathing

This is the same drill described in the rotation section, but now you see how far you can swim on 20 breaths. Remember, this is not a breath-holding contest; in fact, holding your breath for an extended period is not only dangerous but also does not help you swim farther or better.

TO DECREASE DIFFICULTY

• Use fins to prevent that stalling feeling and isolate the catch and pull.
• Use a pull buoy to maintain balance.

Success Check

- You can do the drill without holding your breath but instead exhaling slowly.
- You can make it farther each time you try.

Score Your Success

1 point: You can do 20 breaths, traveling less than 50 yards.

2 points: You can do 20 breaths and travel more than 50 yards.

4 points: You can travel more than 25 yards in 20 strokes and more than 50 yards on 20 breaths.

5–10 points: You can travel more than 30 yards in 20 strokes and more than 75 yards on 20 breaths.

KICKING

As discussed in step 2, the flutter kick is a very important skill, and the challenge now is to apply that skill in a swimming motion—specifically, the freestyle stroke, in which the body is no longer flat on the water. Although you start by kicking with a kickboard, you incorporate rotation when breathing. When done correctly, kicking not only provides propulsive force but also assists with balance. The flutter kick, in particular, uses an alternating leg movement, and the whole leg is moved both up and down to put pressure on the water both on the down stroke of the kick and on the upstroke.

Many novice swimmers have difficulty with this skill because their legs are too rigid and produce no propulsive power. When done properly, the kick's power comes from the hip, and the strong muscles of the lower core are actively engaged. The rest of the leg is kept long and loose, and you are encouraged to think of the knee joint and ankle joint of each leg as being connected by a rubber band. In this way, the kick is more likely to be long and fluid rather than stiff and mechanical.

It is okay to point your toes slightly, but pointing too aggressively (rather than using your ankle's natural flexion) can lead to a rigid and unproductive kick. An unproductive kick can also be caused by having your foot out of the water. Remember, the goal is to exert pressure on the water; generally, therefore, only your heel should break the surface.

MISSTEP

Your kick is rigid and not propulsive.

CORRECTION

Narrow your kick and speed it up just a bit. Remember that a splash indicates simply that the water is absorbing your energy. Think of trying to kick with your feet inside of a bucket or a basketball hoop. Rather than pointing your toes, think about curling them and keeping you knees and ankles "floppy" or loose.

MISSTEP

You go nowhere or even backward when kicking.

CORRECTION

Check your feet and ankles. Are they pointed and rigid? Are they dorsiflexed (in an L shape)? Keep the lower part of your legs loose and your feet *slightly* pointed. Keeping your legs long, with little knee flexion, prevents "bicycling" or pushing at the water. Remember that the kick should come from the hip.

DRILLS FOR KICKING

Kicking is critical to taking pressure off of your shoulders and engaging your core in the swimming motions. The following drills help you to practice your propulsive kick.

Kicking Drill 1   Kickboard

This is a good drill for developing flutter-kick basics. To do it, grab the kickboard at the bottom and extend your arms. Push off of the wall and begin flutter-kicking on your front with your face in the water. Exhale slowly and drop one arm to your side while rotating. This drill is also a good way to practice your breathing; make sure to turn your hip over and catch a quick breath to the side. Recover your hand over the water as usual. At this point, you may feel your hips sink. This is a problem because it disturbs the line of travel and impedes efficiency. Experiment with the amplitude, size, and frequency of your kicks to keep the hips up.

TO INCREASE DIFFICULTY

- Place one hand on the kickboard and kick on your side (right side for 25 yards and left side for 25 yards).
- Eliminate the kickboard and kick in a streamlined position.
- Kick underwater in a streamlined position.

TO DECREASE DIFFICULTY

- Use fins to prevent that stalling feeling and avoid rushing the drill.
- Rest your upper arms across the kickboard by gripping the top to keep your face out of the water. Be aware that doing so may put extra stress on your lower back.
- Use a swimmer's snorkel.

Success Check

- You can keep your face in the water and kick effectively.
- You can breathe to the side rather than lifting your head.

Score Your Success

1 point: You can go somewhere if resting on the kickboard.

2 points: The kickboard is extended, but you need fins.

3 points: You can do very well with the kickboard extended and no fins.

4 points: You can go without the board but need fins

5–7 points: You are an expert, needing neither fins nor board.

Kicking Drill 2　Vertical Kicking

In this drill, which requires deeper water, simply go to a treading-water position and flutter-kick. Most swimmers use their hands for balance. The purpose of the drill is to develop a propulsive kick that is symmetrical.

TO INCREASE DIFFICULTY

- Put your hands on your shoulders with your arms crossed as you kick.
- Put your hands on your head as you kick.
- Put your hands above your head in a streamlined position.

TO DECREASE DIFFICULTY

- Use fins to add surface area.
- Use your hands in a sculling motion to provide lift.
- Use two kickboards for flotation—one in each hand.

Success Check

- You can perform the drill without using your arms.
- You can do the drill for more time on each try.

Score Your Success

1 point: You can tread and vertical-kick with fins.

2 points: You can tread and vertical-kick without fins.

3 points: You can vertical-kick with fins and no hands for 20 seconds.

4 points: You can vertical-kick without fins or hands for 20 seconds.

5 or 6 points: You can streamline-kick vertically with fins for at least 20 seconds. Without using the fins is 6 points.

Kicking Drill 3 Shooters

This drill works on both kicking and body positioning. The object is to sink underwater, achieve a streamlined position, and push off of the wall forcefully. Then start kicking as fast as you can in order to go as far as you can underwater, keeping in mind that of course you will need to come up for air. Remember that your body position dictates your depth; if your head is down you will stay down, but the moment you lift your head you will rise to the surface. Repeat this drill several times to increase your distance traveled from the wall. Exhale in a slow, controlled fashion throughout the movement.

TO INCREASE DIFFICULTY

- Perform this drill for at least 15 yards.

TO DECREASE DIFFICULTY

- Use fins to prevent that stalling feeling and avoid rushing the drill.

Success Check

- You can perform the drill while maintaining a long body line.
- You do not break the surface until you need to breathe.
- You have a powerful kick on both the upstroke and the downstroke.
- You have a great streamline.

Score Your Success

5 points: You can do well with fins for 12.5 yards.

10 points: You can do well without fins for 12.5 yards.

TIMING AND RHYTHM

Putting all of these individual skills together is the last part of the process (figure 3.6). As you can tell from the previous sections, this step has a lot of components; as a result, you need not get frustrated if you don't get it right on the first try. Ideally, the fastest freestyle swimming happens with six kicks per armstroke, in which case you are moving the lower part of your body much faster than the upper part. Try this progression to maximize your chance for success.

Figure 3.6 SYNCHRONIZED KICKING

Preparation

1. From the wall, push off in a streamlined position and begin swimming slowly with just your arms.
2. Establish a comfortable, rhythmic breathing pattern.

Execution

1. Slowly add a flutter kick with just two kicks per stroke. This is almost like the natural counterswing of your body while walking.
2. Increase the frequency of your kicks gradually until you reach six kicks per stroke.

MISSTEP
Your feet go really wide when your breathe.

CORRECTION
This is a common problem when a swimmer lifts the head or fails to leave the leading arm out front and then needs the wide kick to maintain balance. Make sure that you reach out as far as you can with your lead arm and make yourself as long as you can from fingertips to toe tips. Doing so keeps your body on the same line and prevents that out-of-control feeling.

MISSTEP

Your kicking stops altogether when you breathe.

CORRECTION

Slow your kicking to a two-beat kick but try to get three or four small kicks in when you breathe; this approach helps you stay aware of where your feet are and reminds you to keep kicking.

Here are a couple of keys to keep in mind: Your kick should not be too big. A kick that is too big is outside of the drag shadow, which is a column of water that is moving with you and slightly behind your leading edge. Since it is turbulent already, adding propulsion to it will increase velocity. If your kick goes outside of this column of moving water into nonturbulent water, any surfaces past that turbulent or nonturbulant interface produce more drag. Also, make sure not to stop your stroke by overfocusing on counting your kicks; if you do have a pause in your stroke at this stage, make sure that it occurs when both arms are out front. You are in the most streamlined position possible at that point. The drag is minimal compared to the profile for every other part of the movement.

DRILLS FOR TIMING AND RHYTHM

When you walk with good synchronization of movement, it is effortless, and you really don't need to think about it very much. In contrast, swimming is a less natural movement for humans, so we have to learn how to put it all together. The following timing-and-rhythm drills help you get a feel for when to move which body parts and where.

Timing-and-Rhythm Drill 1   Three-Quarters Catch-Up

This is a popular drill for practicing rhythm and timing. Start with the catch-up drill described earlier in this step. Slowly start your lead hand as your other hand catches up, until your hands are passing in front of your head rather than truly catching up. The amount of alteration in rhythm depends on the swimmer, so repeat the drill multiple times to find out what works best for you.

TO INCREASE DIFFICULTY

• Perform six kicks per stroke.

• Go from catch-up to hands opposite each other (i.e., increase the turnover of the arm stroke) and adjust based on feel and distance.

TO DECREASE DIFFICULTY

• Use fins to prevent that stalling feeling and avoid rushing the drill.

• Use a pull buoy to maintain balance.

• Use a swimmer's snorkel.

Success Check

- You can perform the drill while maintaining a long body line.
- You are not letting your hands catch up—but almost.
- You can finish your stroke past your hip.
- Your face is back in the water before you start the pull.

Score Your Success

1 point: You can do the drill but have to rush and need fins.

2 points: You can do the pull drill correctly but need fins.

3 points: You can do the drill correctly for a few strokes.

4 points: You can do the drill correctly for 25 yards with a swimmer's snorkel.

5–10 points: You can do the drill correctly for at least 25 yards (5 points) and perhaps up to 50 yards (10 points). 1 point for each additional 5 yards.

Timing-and-Rhythm Drill 2   2-6 Kicking

This is a progression drill. Start off with a relaxed two-beat kick, then gradually add one kick for each 25 yards until you reach six kicks per stroke. One of the kicking patterns will feel the most relaxed and comfortable to you, and which one it is may change over time. This drill should be repeated often because kick timing changes with stroke efficiency and rate.

TO DECREASE DIFFICULTY

- Use fins to prevent that stalling feeling and avoid rushing the drill.
- Use a swimmer's snorkel.

Success Check

- You can perform the drill while maintaining a long body line.
- You do not make big fountain splashes.
- You find a kicking rhythm that is comfortable.

Score Your Success

5 points: You can do all kicking cycles but feel awkward.

10 points: You find a rhythm that works for you without twisting against yourself.

Backstroke

The modern backstroke was introduced into international competition at the 1900 Olympic Games in Paris (freestyle events were first contested at the 1896 Games). This first appearance of what resembles the modern backstroke led to several technique changes, as well as revised notions of how to swim the stroke most effectively. The original backstroke was performed with the arms straight underwater and somewhat loose on the over-the-water recovery, almost as if it were the front crawl or freestyle turned upside down. Later, Australian swimmers used a bent-arm pull and developed a stroke closer to what is recognized as backstroke today.

The great advantage of backstroke over other strokes is that the swimmer's face is out of the water. In addition, swimmers who master the backstroke develop great balance on the water, which also benefits their freestyle stroke. In this step, you will develop the following skills:

- Horizontal body line
- Rotation on a long axis
- Splashless entry and effective catch
- Pressure on the water throughout the stroke
- Kicking rhythm
- Effective breathing
- Effective timing

Once you have mastered all of these skills, you are well on your way to an effective backstroke.

A good horizontal position is a key element of an effective backstroke and also lays the foundation for applying force to the water to achieve propulsion. As mastered in step 1 (floating on your back), the basic position involves lying on the water with your head, hips, feet, and hands at the surface. As you remain stretched out on the water, ensure that you are comfortable and balanced.

BASIC BACKSTROKE

A good armstroke for the backstroke (figure 4.1) consists of four basic elements that provide the bulk of the propulsive force in swimming: catch, pull, finish (with your palm toward your body, not toward the bottom of the pool), and recovery. At some point when the stroking arm is near vertical, rotate your hand so that your pinkie finger leads the stroke recovery. Remember that as you work on mastering a skill, it is crucial to move in a slow, controlled manner at first. As you may notice, kicking is not mentioned here; this does not mean that you should not kick but simply that you should focus on the skill being described.

Figure 4.1 BASIC BACKSTROKE

Preparation

1. Make sure that the lane is clear and that backstroke flags are in place.
2. Assume a balanced position on your back.

Execution: Catch

1. Beginning with your left hand and arm, rotate the hand so that you pitch the pinkie finger toward the bottom of the pool. Doing so causes you to rotate slightly onto your side.
2. Flex your wrist so that your hand is perpendicular to the direction in which you wish to go.

Follow-Through: Pull

1. The second element is the pull, during which you bend your elbow so that your forearm is also perpendicular to the direction in which you want to go. Keep your elbow away from your body and prevent it from leading the pull.
2. Pull your arm through with your hand and forearm remaining perpendicular to the direction in which you are going.

Finish

1. As you progress through the middle of the stroke— and once your arm is about midway down your body— transition from a pulling motion to a pushing motion, almost as if you were trying to slap your thigh with your hand.

MISSTEP

Your feet sink.

CORRECTION

Use a pull buoy between your thighs to help with balance. You will not need this aid once you develop a good kick.

MISSTEP

You keep your arm straight and locked throughout the pull as it makes a big circle.

CORRECTION

Think of the motion as grabbing an armful of water and pushing it to your feet, pushing down as if trying to slap your thigh. This cue will allow you to bend at the elbow.

MISSTEP

You finish the pull with your palm down.

CORRECTION

Think of trying to slap your thigh with your hand. Since water cannot be compressed, you won't actually be able to do it, but the image helps you remember to finish the stroke.

MULTIPLE-STROKE BACKSTROKE

Once you have gone through one stroke cycle—one right arm and one left arm—it is time to put together multiple stroke cycles. Unlike the "catching up" pattern of freestyle, in backstroke your hands should always be at opposite ends of the stroke pattern (figure 4.2).

For safety, practice this skill in a pool that is long enough for seven to ten strokes and equipped with backstroke flags. The flags are placed 5 yards from the end of the pool, and most swimmers can take two or three strokes after passing beneath them before reaching the wall.

Figure 4.2 Multiple-stroke backstroke.

Make sure that the lane is clear and equipped with backstroke flags. Assume a balanced position on your back. Push off in a streamlined position with your face out of the water and begin stroking with whichever arm is most comfortable for you; take seven to ten strokes. Repeat this process several times, trying to get farther down the pool with the same number of strokes.

MISSTEP

You make a lot of splashing and thrashing movements.

CORRECTION

Many swimmers tend to rush the arm to the top of the stroke, which causes excessive splash. Remember that the goal here is to slow down the armstroke in order to have a splashless entry.

MISSTEP

You continually pull a curtain of water into your face.

CORRECTION

As you finish the stroke, rotate your hip on the same side as your stroking arm and the shoulder of your stroking arm toward the sky. This action allows you to exit the water cleanly with your thumb first; if it is done slowly enough, only a little water will drip off of your arm and hand.

DRILLS FOR ARMSTROKES

Armstroke drills help you ensure that you perform a proper entry, catch, and pull by isolating the movements so that you can focus on just one portion of the stroke. The three drills presented here also help you with rotation and rhythm.

Armstroke Drill 1   Six-Kick Switch

This drill helps you with armstrokes, balance, and timing. To perform the drill, begin kicking on your back with both hands above your head. Turn over slightly to your side and pull one arm down to the side. Hold your position on the side—with one arm extended and its pinkie finger down and your other arm flat against your side—for six kicks. Then pull again as your hands switch places. Repeat the drill for the length of the pool.

TO INCREASE DIFFICULTY

- Close your hand into a fist to ensure that you get a catch with your forearm as well as your hand.

TO DECREASE DIFFICULTY

- Use fins to prevent that stalling feeling and isolate the catch and pull.

Success Check

- You can perform the drill while maintaining a long body line.
- You are not breaking the surface or too deep after the first pullout when you begin your first stroke. Your body should just break the surface at the same time that the stroke starts.

Score Your Success

1 point: You can do it with fins for a few strokes.

2 points: You can do it with fins for the length of the pool.

3 points: You can do 7 or more strokes with no fins.

4 points: You can do 10 or more strokes with no fins.

5 points: You can go the length of the pool with no fins.

7–10 points: You can go at least half of the pool length with your hands balled into fists (7 points) or the full length of the pool (10 points).

Armstroke Drill 2   Hesitation

In this drill, you stop the recovery midway through, when your arm is out of the water and vertical. When you stop the recovery motion, rotate your hand and then continue the recovery, being sure that your hand enters the water pinkie first with little or no splash. Hesitate for just a second or two—just enough to stop the motion of your arm toward your head.

TO INCREASE DIFFICULTY

- In order to ensure the hesitation, rotate your hand and your entire arm at the top of the recovery two or three times. This is the time to reposition your hand from thumb out to pinkie out.

TO DECREASE DIFFICULTY

- Use fins to prevent that stalling feeling in the forward motion and to isolate the catch and pull.

Success Check

- You can remain in the hesitation part of the drill for a few seconds with your shoulder and arm perpendicular to the surface of the water.
- You are not breaking the surface or too deep after the first pullout.
- You do not splash the water by rushing to the next stroke after the hesitation portion of the drill.

Score Your Success

1 point: You can complete four stroke cycles with fins.

2 points: You can complete five or more stroke cycles with fins.

3 points: You can complete four stroke cycles without fins.

4 points: You can complete five or more stroke cycles without fins.

5–8 points: You can go for least 25 yards without fins and without stopping.

Armstroke Drill 3   Double-Arm Backstroke

This is a classic drill that helps you keep your hand on the same plane as your shoulders during the armstroke. To do it, start kicking with your hands at your sides. Simultaneously raise both arms out of the water, with your thumbs exiting first, then rotate your hands to enter the water pinkies first. Your hands should enter a little more than shoulder-width apart. Bend your elbows slightly while catching the water with your hands and pulling down toward your thighs. Make sure to finish with your palms flat against your thighs rather than down toward the pool bottom.

TO INCREASE DIFFICULTY

- Ball your hands into fists.

TO DECREASE DIFFICULTY

- Use fins to prevent that stalling feeling and isolate the catch and pull.

Success Check

- You can perform the drill while maintaining a long body line.
- You can keep your elbows out away from your body.
- You are not breaking the surface or too deep after the first pullout.
- Your hands do not break the surface as you pull down.
- You finish the stroke with your palms toward your sides, not toward the pool bottom.

Score Your Success

1 point: You can complete four stroke cycles with fins.

2 points: You can complete five or more stroke cycles with fins.

3 points: You can complete four stroke cycles without fins.

4 points: You can complete five or more stroke cycles without fins.

5–8 points: You can go at least 25 yards without fins and without stopping.

ROTATION

Because the backstroke is driven by your legs and hips, you must use your core muscles to turn your hip and shoulder over as one piece in order to perform an effective catch and pull. Ideally, you get a deep, effective catch and pull by using your body for rotation (figure 4.3) rather than "faking it" by finishing the stroke with your palm under your hip to force the hip over. The latter approach also forces you to lift your arm all the way back to the surface and creates extra drag. Rotation also reduces drag in another way—by reducing your cross-sectional area on the water.

In addition, rotation in the backstroke helps you keep your upper arms in line with your collarbones; imagine a single line extending from elbow to elbow and passing straight through your shoulders. What proper alignment through proper body rotation means for the backstroke is that you never reach behind yourself, which is a good thing since little or no power can be generated there. Reaching behind is similar to trying to push yourself up out of the water with your back to the wall and your hands on the deck. You may be able to do it if you are really strong, but the effort would lead to shoulder injury over the long run.

When doing any of these drills or skills, make sure that the backstroke flags are in place or that you have a partner to stop you before you get to a wall.

Figure 4.3 **BACKSTROKE ROTATION**

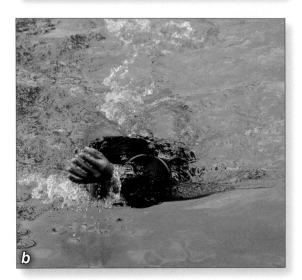

Preparation

1. Make sure that the lane is clear and that backstroke flags are in place.

Execution

1. Push off on your back and begin rotating to the side of your nonstroking hand.
2. As you pull with your submerged hand and arm, your opposite arm should move out slightly to the catch position.
3. As your submerged arm finishes the pull, use your core muscles and your kicking motion for hip drive and rotate your body.
4. Your first-stroke arm and shoulder should now have rotated to the top of the water and out as your opposite hand and arm enter the catch phase.
5. Recover the hand that just finished its stroke with the thumb first, then repeat the cycle.

MISSTEP

You sink when you rotate from side to side.

CORRECTION

Put on fins for propulsion until you develop a better kicking motion.

MISSTEP

You can't keep your head still while rotating.

CORRECTION

Lay your goggles on top of your forehead without securing the strap around your head. In order to keep the goggles from falling off, you will have to keep your head still!

DRILLS FOR ROTATION

The following drills help you maintain proper body and head positioning while working on your rotation. Keep in mind that each drill may involve an overcorrection of a typical flaw; when you transition back to swimming the stroke, you can smooth everything out to make each motion fluid.

Rotation Drill 1   Shoulder Roll

This position drill helps you become aware of how your hip and shoulder are connected for the stroke and how to use your core muscles to drive rotation. To do the drill, push off of the wall and begin kicking on your back with your hands at your sides. Once you are comfortable, roll one shoulder up to your chin, making sure that the same-side hip turns with the shoulder. Return to the neutral position on the water and repeat with the opposite shoulder. Go through several cycles of this pattern to ensure that you are comfortable with rotating on the long axis of your body without sinking.

TO INCREASE DIFFICULTY

- Perform six kicks per stroke as part of the stroke mentione d in the introduction.
- Place the goggles on your forehead with no strap.

TO DECREASE DIFFICULTY

- Use fins to prevent that stalling feeling and avoid rushing the drill.
- Use your hands in a sculling motion for balance.

(continued)

Rotation Drill 1 *(continued)*

Success Check

- You can perform the drill while maintaining a long body line.
- You can roll each shoulder out of the water.
- You are not breaking the surface or too deep after the first pullout.
- You can bring each shoulder up to your chin while keeping your head steady.

1 point: You can do the drill with fins, but it is very challenging and you can do only two cycles before stopping.

2 points: You can do the drill with fins for 25 yards, but it is still a struggle.

3 points: You can do the drill easily with fins.

4–7 points: You can do the drill easily without fins for at least half of the pool length.

Rotation Drill 2　One-Arm Backstroke

This drill is very similar to the one-arm freestyle drill. To do it, push off on your back and keep one arm at your side. Begin stroking with the other arm and be sure to rotate to both sides. Swimmers often find it easier to rotate to one side than to the other, so this drill may take some practice.

TO INCREASE DIFFICULTY

- Perform six kicks per stroke.

TO DECREASE DIFFICULTY

- Use fins to prevent that stalling feeling and avoid rushing the drill.
- Use your nonstroking hand for balance by sculling.

Success Check

- You can perform the drill while maintaining a long body line.
- You can rotate your body to both the stroking side and the non-stroking side.
- You are not breaking the surface or too deep after the first pullout.
- Your recovering arm does not pull up a curtain of water.
- You can do the drill on both sides.

Score Your Success

1 point: You can do the drill with fins, but it is very challenging, and you can do only two cycles before stopping.

2 points: You can do the drill with fins for 25 yards, but it is still a struggle.

3 points: You can do the drill easily with fins.

4–7 points: You can do the drill easily without fins for at least half of the pool length.

Rotation Drill 3   Slap Your Thigh

This drill is more advanced than the others and strongly emphasizes rotation on the recovery. To do it, push off of the wall on your back in a streamlined position with your hands extended beyond your head as described in step 1. Begin a pull with one arm, leaving the other arm in place beyond your head. As you recover the stroking arm, stop when it is vertical, then bring it back down with the palm on your thigh before initiating the recovery again—only this time recovering all the way through to the entry. If you rotated over—as in the spine being an axis and the arc of rotation includes the hip and shoulder together in the same plane at a fixed distance—your hand and thigh should be at or above the water's surface. As you begin the full recovery, begin the same motion sequence with your other arm.

TO INCREASE DIFFICULTY

- Perform six kicks per stroke.

TO DECREASE DIFFICULTY

- Use fins to prevent that stalling feeling and avoid rushing the drill.
- Use your nonstroking hand for balance by sculling.

Success Check

- You can perform the drill while maintaining a long body line.
- Your hand and elbow stay on the same plane, as if you were pushing an armful of water to your feet.
- Your elbow stays out away from your body.
- Your upper arm and collarbones all stay on the same line.
- You are not breaking the surface or too deep after the first pullout.
- You finish the stroke with your palm on your thigh rather than toward the pool bottom.

Score Your Success

1 point: You can do the drill with fins, but it is very challenging and you can do only two cycles before stopping.

2 points: You can do the drill with fins for 25 yards, but it is still a struggle.

3 points: You can do the drill easily with fins.

4–7 points: You can do the drill easily without fins for at least half of the pool length.

KICKING

When done correctly, kicking not only provides propulsive force but also helps you with balance. The kick used for the backstroke is the flutter kick (figure 4.4). It features alternating leg movement, and the whole leg is moved up and down to put pressure on the water both on the downstroke and on the upstroke.

This kick is generally the same one used in freestyle swimming but with a few minor points of difference. As in freestyle, think of each leg's knee joint and ankle joint as being connected by a rubber band. In this way, the kick is more likely to be long and fluid rather than stiff and mechanical. In another pitfall, many swimmers tend to "paw" at the water by emphasizing the downkick and neglecting the upkick or by raising the leg too high out of the water.

Figure 4.4 **BACKSTROKE KICKING**

a

b

c

Preparation

1. Make sure that the lane is clear and the backstroke flags are in place.

Execution

1. Lie on the water in the neutral position.
2. Begin the flutter-kicking motion.
3. Keep your legs long and loose and feel the pressure on both the tops and the bottoms of your feet.
4. Use your whole leg to kick rather than just the lower portion (below the knee).
5. Curl your toes while keeping your ankles and knees loose.

MISSTEP

Your kick is too big and makes a lot of splash.

CORRECTION

Think of your toes just flicking the top of the water. A good visualization for many people is to pretend that a soccer ball is floating on the water and you are just trying to kick it with the top of your foot.

MISSTEP

You go nowhere or even backward when kicking.

CORRECTION

Check your feet and ankles. Are they pointed and rigid? Are they dorsiflexed (in an L shape)? Keep the lower part of your leg loose and think of curling your toes rather than pointing them.

DRILLS FOR KICKING

To practice developing a propulsive kick, try the following drills. Remember that the leg movements should be long and fluid.

Kicking Drill 1   Kickboard

This is a good drill for developing flutter-kick basics on your back. To do it, grab the kickboard at the bottom and extend your arms down this time. Push off of the wall and begin flutter-kicking on your back with the kickboard down across your upper legs. Experiment with the amplitude or size of the kick, as well as the frequency. Only your toes should break the surface—not your knees. If you do it incorrectly or "bicycle," your knees will bounce off of the kickboard. In this case, remember that you just need to have your toes touch the surface.

TO INCREASE DIFFICULTY

- Eliminate the kickboard and kick in a streamlined position.
- Kick underwater in a streamlined position.

TO DECREASE DIFFICULTY

- Use fins to prevent stalling and keep your ankles flexible.

(continued)

Kicking Drill 1 *(continued)*

Success Check

- You can perform the drill while maintaining a long body line.
- You can keep your knees from hitting the kickboard, but your toes break the surface.
- You are not breaking the surface or too deep after the first pullout.
- You can put pressure on the water with both the tops and the bottoms of your feet.

Score Your Success

1 point: You can go somewhere, but the kickboard dances around while bouncing off of your knees.

2 points: The kickboard stays still, but you have to use fins.

3 points: You can do very well without fins, and the kickboard stays still.

4 points: You can go without the board but need fins.

5–7 points: You are an expert, needing neither fins nor board.

Kicking Drill 2   Vertical Kicking

In this drill, which requires deeper water, simply go to a treading-water position and flutter-kick. Most swimmers use their hands for balance. The purpose of the drill is to develop a propulsive kick that is symmetrical. You can do this drill as vertical kicking with one hand up out of the water, then switch to having the other hand up after six kicks.

TO INCREASE DIFFICULTY

- Put your hands on your shoulders with your arms crossed as you kick.
- Put your hands on your head as you kick.
- Put your hands above your head in a streamlined position.

TO DECREASE DIFFICULTY

- Use fins to add surface area.
- Use your hands in a sculling motion to provide lift.
- Use two kickboards for flotation—one in each hand.

Success Check

- You can perform the drill while maintaining a long body line.
- You can maintain a vertical position in the same spot in the water with one arm out.
- You are not breaking the surface or too deep after the first pullout.
- You can switch arms without sinking.
- You can perform this skill for more than 10 seconds.

Score Your Success

1 point: You can tread and vertical-kick with fins.

2 points: You can tread and vertical-kick without fins.

3 points: You can vertical-kick with fins and no hands for 20 seconds.

4 points: You can vertical-kick without fins and no hands for 20 seconds.

5 or 6 points: You can streamline-kick vertically with fins for at least 20 seconds.

7–10 points: You can streamline-kick vertically without fins for at least 20 seconds.

Kicking Drill 3   Shooters

This drill helps you develop both your kicking and your body positioning. To perform the drill, sink underwater, achieve a streamlined position on your back, and push off of the wall forcefully. Then start kicking as fast as you can in order to go as far as you can underwater, keeping in mind that of course you will need to come up for air.

Remember that your body position dictates your depth; if your head is down you will stay down, but the moment you lift your head or look toward your feet you will rise to the surface. Many swimmers use a nose clip to prevent water from going up the nose; it can also be prevented by exhaling slowly through your nose. Repeat this drill several times to increase your distance from the wall.

TO INCREASE DIFFICULTY

- Extend the distance that you shoot (notify the lifeguard that you are working on this skill).
- Wear old tennis shoes to increase resistance.

TO DECREASE DIFFICULTY

- Use fins to prevent that stalling feeling and avoid rushing the drill.

Success Check

- You can perform the drill while maintaining a long body line.
- You are not breaking the surface or too deep after the first pullout.
- You keep your rib cage up toward the sky or ceiling, very rigid, and streamlined.

Score Your Success

3 points: You can do it with fins for half of the pool length.

5 points: You can do it with fins for more than half of the pool length.

7 points: You can do it without fins for half of the pool length.

10 points: You can do it without fins for more than half of the pool length.

TIMING AND RHYTHM

Putting all of these individual skills together is the last part of the process. As you can tell from the previous sections, this step involves a number of components; as a result, you need not get frustrated if you don't get it right on the first try. Generally, the fastest backstroke swimming happens with six kicks per armstroke, in which case you are moving the lower part of your body much faster than the upper part. Try this progression to maximize your chance for success (figure 4.5).

Figure 4.5 BACKSTROKE TIMING AND RHYTHM

Preparation

1. From the wall, push off in a streamlined position and begin swimming slowly with just your arms.
2. Establish a comfortable, rhythmic breathing pattern.

Execution

1. Slowly add a flutter kick with two kicks per stroke, just using your feet to help your hips and provide balance.
2. Increase the frequency of your kicks gradually until you reach six kicks per stroke.

MISSTEP

Your feet go really wide.

CORRECTION

This is a common problem when swimmers use their feet for balance or underreach by being out too wide on the entry. Correct this misstep by entering at shoulder-width or maybe a little wider.

MISSTEP

Your kicking stops altogether, and your feet sink.

CORRECTION

Slow your kicking to a two-beat kick but try to get a few more kicks in as you get more comfortable. The backstroke is a leg-driven and hip-driven stroke, which means that rotation comes from both the core muscles and the kick. Using you core to rotate first is key; then add the kicking to synchronize your movements.

Here are a couple of keys to keep in mind: Your kick should not be too big. Fluid mechanics tells us the displaced water around the body will create what is called a drag shadow. You can think of this as a moving column of water. As the vortices are shed off the sides and back of the body, this turbulent water will almost give you a bit of lift when kicking force is applied. The edge of the drag shadow is at the interface between the turbulent and nonturbulent water. Any trailing body parts extending beyond that area act to increase the cross-sectional profile of displaced water and increase drag as a resistive force exponentially. Also, make sure not to stop your stroke by overfocusing on counting your kicks; if you do have a pause in your stroke at this stage, make sure that it occurs when your arms are opposite each other.

DRILLS FOR TIMING AND RHYTHM

As with all strokes, good timing and rhythm are key elements of the backstroke. Unlike freestyle, in which your hands pass above your head and almost "catch up" to each other, backstroke is a hands-opposite type of stroke. That is, one hand should be entering the water as the other hand is exiting. The following drills help you develop a good timing pattern for a smooth and rhythmic stroke

Timing-and-Rhythm Drill 1   Switch

In this easy drill, you simply hold one arm out and above in the catch position and the other arm down at your thigh. You then say *switch*—first on a count of five seconds, then on a count of four, then three, and so on, until it becomes a smooth stroke.

TO INCREASE DIFFICULTY

- Perform six kicks per stroke.

TO DECREASE DIFFICULTY

- Use fins to prevent that stalling feeling and avoid rushing the drill.

Success Check

- You can perform the drill while maintaining a long body line.
- You can kick on your side and hold a balanced position.
- You are not breaking the surface or too deep after the first pullout.
- You can synchronize your kicking and pulling motions so that you are not twisting against yourself.

Score Your Success

1 point: You use fins.

2 points: You scull to maintain balance.

5 points: You can perform the drill by dropping to one on the switch count without interruption or hesitation in your stroke.

Timing-and-Rhythm Drill 2   3-5 Switch

This timing-and-rhythm drill also works on positioning. It is the same as the freestyle 3-5 Switch drill except that here it uses the backstroke. To perform the drill, push off of the wall, take three strokes, and at the end of the last stroke keep your lead arm forward as your trailing arm finishes the stroke at your thigh. Hold that position for five kicks before taking three more strokes and repeating the same movement. The odd number of strokes means that you will kick on different sides.

TO INCREASE DIFFICULTY

- Perform six kicks per stroke.

TO DECREASE DIFFICULTY

- Use fins to prevent that stalling feeling and avoid rushing the drill.

Success Check

- You can perform the drill while maintaining a long body line.
- You can hold your body position steady for five kicks.
- You can do three perfect pulls that are splashless and maintain rotation.
- You are not breaking the surface or too deep after the first pullout.
- You can perform the switch without splashing.

Score Your Success

1 point: You use fins.

2 points: You scull to maintain balance.

5 points: You can perform the drill for at least 25 yards with no fins.

SUCCESS SUMMARY

The backstroke is very similar to the freestyle in the sense that it relies a great deal on the core. It differs mainly in being driven more by the lower core of the body rather than being something that one can "muscle through" with just the upper body. It is wise to have your instructor or coach record video of your swimming and evaluate your stroke in order to ensure that you are doing what you think you are doing—and to help you make any needed adjustments.

SCORE YOUR SUCCESS

If you scored at least 51 points, then you have completed this step. If you scored 52 to 75 points, then you are well on your way and have the potential to develop your swimming stroke even further. If you scored more than 76 points, then you have mastered the key elements for taking your swimming to the next level.

Armstroke Drills

1.	Six-Kick Switch	____ out of 10
2.	Hesitation	____ out of 8
3.	Double-Arm Backstroke	____ out of 8

Rotation Drills

1.	Shoulder Roll	____ out of 7
2.	One-Arm Backstroke	____ out of 7
3.	Slap Your Thigh	____ out of 7

Breathing Drill

1.	Backstroke Breathing Pattern	____ out of 5

Kicking Drills

1.	Kickboard	____ out of 7
2.	Vertical Kicking	____ out of 10
3.	Shooters	____ out of 10

Timing-and-Rhythm Drills

1.	Switch	____ out of 5
2.	3-5 Switch	____ out of 5
	Total	____ **out of 89**

Breaststroke

The breaststroke has gone through many phases and holds a place in many cultures around the world. Some theorize that it was originated by mimicking the motions of a frog, though the modern version differs somewhat in terms of the kick. In any case, it can be traced back at least to the Stone Age, when cave paintings were made in what is now western Egypt to depict people using the stroke. The breaststroke was also the only stroke used for the first recorded crossing of the English Channel by a swimmer.

There are several advantages: It is possible to breathe after every stroke, see where you are going, and use the stroke for survival and safety once you know how to do this stroke effectively. Though it is technically the slowest of the four competitive strokes, its subtleties and nuances make it arguably the most complex as well. Though everyone can learn to do the breaststroke—and should, since a slower variant of it is essential in swimming long distances when necessary—learning to swim it fast takes a great deal of patience and time.

Breaststroke and butterfly are considered "short-axis" strokes but are really timing-and-rhythm strokes. Granted, you do rotate on a shorter axis (i.e., through the chest, laterally) rather than on a long axis (down the spine), but the most important elements to keep in mind with this stroke are common to all of the strokes:

- Good body position
- Effective catch
- Pressure on the water throughout the stroke
- Kicking rhythm
- Effective breathing
- Effective timing

Once you have mastered all of these components, you are well on your way to an effective breaststroke.

The breaststroke is the only one of the four competitive strokes that derives its propulsive force equally from the pull and the kick; therefore, you should give equal attention to both elements. This double focus is one factor that makes the breaststroke so elusive for some swimmers. At any level, if you look across the race pool, you will find a greater variety of styles being used for the breaststroke than for any other competitive stroke. Some swimmers use a wider pull or kick, whereas others use a quicker stroke rate and still others a longer rate. Bottom line: there is no agreed-upon best way to do this stroke.

As with the other strokes, however, there are certain basic movements that provide propulsive force and minimize drag. More specifically, though it is true that you can have a weaker kick in the freestyle or backstroke and still muscle your way through; the same cannot be said of the breaststroke. Therefore, the first element to focus on in the breaststroke is a good kick.

BREASTSTROKE KICK

The following skills and drills will help you master what is the most complex of strokes: the breaststroke. The first of these skills is mastering the breaststroke kick (figure 5.1).

Figure 5.1 **BREASTSTROKE KICK**

Preparation

1. Make sure the area is clear and you have ample space to perform the skill.
2. Start in the horizontal, flat balanced position.

Execution

1. From the horizontal start position, draw the heels up toward the butt.
2. Point the feet and toes in opposite directions away from the midline of the body.
3. Push the heels out while keeping the knees tucked in.
4. Sweep the heels together while pushing against the water with the insides of the calves and the instep of the foot.
5. Hold the position, glide, and then repeat.

MISSTEP

You draw the knees outside before the heels.

CORRECTION

Leading with the knees causes you to wedge the water with the whole leg and places an increased stress on the hips. Instead, think of the knees as being separated by the width of just your hands. Alternately, placing a small buoy higher above the knees when kicking during the breaststroke will accomplish the same thing.

Many swimmers experience the following problems in kicking with the breaststroke. To avoid these common mistakes, review the drills from step 2.

- Kicking "out" as if doing a side kick rather than anchoring the instep and pushing
- Bringing the heels up either too far or not far enough
- Kicking with the toes pointed
- Drawing out with the knees rather than keeping them in
- Keeping the legs together
- Not controlling the core and thus making the finish more of a dolphin kick

Keep these pitfalls in mind in order to avoid later problems that can result from the lack of an effective propulsive kick.

DRILLS FOR KICKING

As mentioned in step 2 (manipulating the water), a good propulsive breaststroke kick is all about putting pressure on the water with the legs from the knee down. For a refresher, practice the following drills.

Kicking Drill 1   Wall Kick

Begin by standing near the pool wall in water that is at least chest deep with your back touching the wall. Starting with your right leg, draw the heel up with the knee still touching the wall in the dorsiflexed or L position. Once your thigh is parallel to the bottom of the pool, stop raising the leg.

While in this position, slide your heel out and away from the centerline of your body while keeping your knee in the same place. This action may seem awkward at first. The key is to make sure that your heel is farther from the center of your body than your knee is. You may need to use the wall for balance.

Once your foot is in position, push the instep in a sweeping motion down toward the bottom of the pool. You have succeeded when you can feel pressure from the water on your instep and on the inside of your calf. Once you have succeeded with your right foot, try this same motion with your left foot. Once you are comfortable with this motion, try both together.

(continued)

Kicking Drill 1 *(continued)*

TO INCREASE DIFFICULTY

- Try the drill with your eyes closed.
- Find deeper water and apply the same kick while facing the wall.

TO DECREASE DIFFICULTY

- Turn and face the wall so that you can look at your leg position.

Success Check

- You can feel pressure on your instep and on the inside of your calf when using your right leg.
- You can feel pressure on your instep and on the inside of your calf when using your left leg.
- You can push with an effective kick with both legs at same time while keeping your knees no more than 12 inches (~30 cm) apart.
- You feel your body lift slightly out of the water.

Score Your Success

1 point: You can do one leg at a time.

3 points: You can do both legs at the same time.

5 points: You can feel a lift when kicking with both legs at the same time.

Once you feel an effective push with your lower body, it is time to start working on applying this force horizontally rather than vertically.

Kicking Drill 2   Moving Through the Water

Now that you feel the pressure on the water, it is time to ensure that it is propulsive pressure by moving through the water. The next part of the progression calls for you to lie on your back in the neutral position described in step 1 with your hands at your sides for balance. Draw your heels up. Once your heels are close to your hips, rotate your heels out wider than your knees and then sweep your heels together. Your lower legs and feet should be dorsiflexed or in an L position. Squeeze your ankles together and point your toes while finishing the kick.

Remember that these motions are more about pressure than about speed or strength. Once you complete one kick, return to the neutral position and let your momentum fade. Repeat the same motion until you are comfortable with it.

Important note! You will not be able to see where you are going during this drill. Make sure that the backstroke flags in place—five yards from the wall—or have your coach or instructor stop you when necessary!

TO INCREASE DIFFICULTY

- Place a kickboard across the upper part of your legs to prevent your upper legs from coming out of the water.
- Place a pull buoy between your legs, slightly above your mid-thighs, to ensure that your knees stay together.

TO DECREASE DIFFICULTY

- Use two kickboards—one in each hand—for balance.
- Use a slight sculling motion to provide a little propulsion at the same time.

Success Check

- You can push with an effective kick with both legs while keeping your knees no more than 12 inches (30 cm) apart.
- You can go 25 yards on your back with ease.

Score Your Success

1 point: You can go 10 yards.

3 points: You can go 25 yards.

5 points: You can go 25 yards in 15 or more kicks.

7 points: You can go 25 yards in fewer than 15 kicks.

Kicking Drill 3   Kicking on Your Front

The next drill for building an effective breaststroke kick involves transferring the back kick from the neutral position to the front. Remember, once your heels are close to your hips, rotate your heels out so that they are wider than your knees, then sweep them together. Your lower legs and feet should be dorsiflexed or in an L position. Squeeze your ankles together and point your toes while finishing the kick. Do this drill first with your hands at your sides for balance, then switch to a streamlined position. Repeat the same motion until you are comfortable with it.

TO INCREASE DIFFICULTY

- Stay in a streamlined position.
- Place a pull buoy between your legs, slightly above mid-thigh, to ensure that your knees stay together.

TO DECREASE DIFFICULTY

- Use a kickboard out front or even lie on it.
- Use a slight sculling motion to provide a little propulsion at the same time.

(continued)

Kicking Drill 3 *(continued)*

Success Check

- You can push with an effective kick with both legs while keeping your knees no more than 12 inches (30 cm) apart.
- You can go 25 yards on your front with ease.

THE PULL

The second propulsive element of the breaststroke is the pull (figure 5.2). Unlike freestyle and backstroke, each of these movements is independent of the other; therefore, timing is crucial. First, focus on developing a really good breaststroke catch-and-pull phase. The difference is that the hands are not stacked one on top of the other as in the preceding skill. The catch and the pull are two parts of the same motion. The release from the pull position is achieved by bringing the elbows together under the body while simultaneously moving the hands forward.

Here is an effective trick for thinking about these movements together. Imagine that you are scraping cake batter out of a bowl with your pinkie fingers, then pushing it to someone else. Your hands accelerate throughout the catch-and-pull phase until reaching the neutral position again. Your hands should *never* go past your shoulders. If they do, you will have to bring them forward, making a propulsive movement in a direction opposite of the way you are swimming. You will then have to start again after this motion makes you stop, thus requiring more energy to accelerate.

Figure 5.2 BREASTSTROKE PULL

Preparation

1. Make sure that you have enough space to perform the drill.
2. Lie in the neutral position on your front with your arms extended and your palms down—almost in a streamlined position.

Execution

1. Initiate the catch movement by sweeping your hands out slightly past your shoulders while pitching your fingers down toward the pool bottom.

2. Your torso and arms should make almost a Y shape when viewed from the top. As your fingers pitch down, your elbows bend slightly to get your forearms into a more vertical position and put additional pressure on the water.

3. Before your hands pass your elbows in the elbow-up-and-hand-down position, stop putting pressure on the water.

4. Collapse your elbows together as your hands push forward.

5. Make sure that your hands accelerate through the movement back to the streamlined position.

MISSTEP

You pull too wide with your elbows straight and your palms out.

CORRECTION

Remember to pitch your fingers down and catch the water. Sweep out as if using a sculling motion, but here the goal is to wrap your fingers down and use your palm to put pressure on the water.

MISSTEP

Your hands come past your shoulders.

CORRECTION

Think of releasing the water earlier or even touching your elbows together under your chest. Doing so helps ensure that your hands do not come past your shoulders on the pull.

DRILLS FOR BREASTSTROKE PULL

The pull in the breaststroke is just as important as the kick—and more important for some swimmers who are not as good at the kick portion. To develop an effective pull, it is helpful to isolate this part of the overall stroke. More specifically, the pitch of your hand and your elbow positioning are just as important here as they are in the other strokes. The elbows-up position allows you to pull with more than just your hand. Use the following drills to develop a pull with good propulsive force.

Pull Drill 1   Breaststroke Pull With Freestyle Kick

This drill isolates the pull by using an easier kick and alleviating timing concerns. To perform the drill, lie on your front and kick freestyle with your hands out front. For every six kicks, perform one breaststroke pull.

TO INCREASE DIFFICULTY

• Kick faster—eight times or more per stroke.

TO DECREASE DIFFICULTY

• Use fins to prevent stalling.
• Use a pull buoy and do not kick at all.

Success Check

- You can feel the water on both your hands and your forearms.
- You can go 25 yards on your front in nine pulls with ease.

Score Your Success

1 point: You can go 10 yards.

3 points: You can go 25 yards.

5 points: You can go 25 yards in 10 or more pulls.

7 points: You can go 25 yards in nine or fewer pulls.

Pull Drill 2   Tennis Ball or Fist

To do this drill, hold a tennis ball in each hand or at least make sure that each hand is closed in a tight fist. Perform the same action as in the preceding drill but without using your hands as a propulsive surface.

TO INCREASE DIFFICULTY

- Kick faster—eight times or more per stroke.

TO DECREASE DIFFICULTY

- Use paddles or open the hands up a bit and just curl the fingers instead of holding tennis balls.

Success Check

- You can feel the water on both your hands and your forearms.
- You can go 25 yards on your front in nine pulls with ease.

Score Your Success

1 point: You can go 10 yards.

3 points: You can go 25 yards.

5 points: You can go 25 yards in 13 or more pulls.

7 points: You can go 25 yards in 12 or fewer pulls.

BREATHING

One of the many advantages of the breaststroke is that you can breathe on every stroke. The exact timing of this breath is an important part of the rhythm of the breaststroke (figure 5.3). As a result, before you start to put it all together for a complete breaststroke, it is a good idea to practice your breathing in isolation. While performing the following drills, lift your head to breathe; the key is to do so at the right time and in the right manner. With the other pressures of laminar flow of water against the chest providing lift on the water, this movement should be sufficient to get your mouth and nose out of the water. Some swimmers will be higher and others lower; it is very specific to each swimmer.

Figure 5.3 BREASTSTROKE BREATHING

a

b

Preparation

1. Lie on the water in the neutral front position.
2. Perform one kick and wait for a full count of two seconds.

Execution

1. Sweep out with your hands. Wait to breathe until you are at the point when your elbows are bent. Breathing occurs in mid to late stroke for a reason: If there is to be a pause in the stroke, it should be just before an acceleration.
2. Instead of lifting your head per se, use the outsweep to generate lift so that all you need is a simple forward push of your chin.
3. Breathe out while your face is in the water.

MISSTEP

You breathe too late and your hand stops under your chin.

CORRECTION

Think about trying to quickly touch your elbows together under your chest. This will get your hands moving forward and force you to breathe a little earlier.

MISSTEP

You push down with the palms of your hands and your hips sink.

CORRECTION

Think about where your fingertips are. They need to be down for the most part to pull forward and not push down.

DRILL FOR BREATHING

Breathing in the breaststroke is really a study in keeping that balanced developed in the first few steps. You know from earlier steps that head position is important. The following drills will help you establish a good head position and help with breathing.

Breathing Drill   Tennis Ball 2

This drill helps you maintain proper head position while going to get air or breathing in breaststroke. To perform the drill, place a tennis ball beneath your chin and hold it to your chest. This action keeps your neck in line and prevents you from coming up too high when you breathe. Swim the regular breaststroke and try breathing both earlier in the stroke and later in the stroke to find out which works best for you. Avoid pushing down on the water with your palms.

TO INCREASE DIFFICULTY

- Leave your face in the water for one or two stroke cycles.

TO DECREASE DIFFICULTY

- Put on fins and use a dolphin kick rather than a breaststroke kick.

Success Check

- You can breathe on every stroke without losing the tennis ball.
- You can go 25 yards with a breaststroke kick while keeping the tennis ball in place.

Score Your Success

1 point: You can go 10 yards.

3 points: You can go 25 yards.

5 points: You can go 25 yards without losing the ball.

7 points: You can go 50 yards without losing the ball.

TIMING AND RHYTHM

Timing is crucial in both the breaststroke and the butterfly but is most important in the breaststroke. To work on your timing, you can use a few simple drills that emphasize it. The secret to the breaststroke hinges on the fact that half of its propulsive force comes from the kick and the other half from the pull. The key is not to do both at the same time. The proper rhythm is one kick, one pull and breath, and a return to the stretched-out position.

DRILLS FOR TIMING AND RHYTHM

Because propulsion in the breaststroke derives equally from the kick and the pull, it is crucial to maximize the efficiency of each element. Get it wrong and you end up being very slow. The key is to make sure that you do not kick when pulling and vice versa. The following drills include some overcorrections of typical problems but should help you separate the two movements so that you can develop a good rhythm.

Timing-and-Rhythm Drill 1   Two-Hippopotamus Breaststroke

This is a slow drill that helps you with your timing. It is performed by pushing off of the wall in the streamlined position. Do one breaststroke kick, then wait while counting "one hippopotamus . . . two hippopotamus." Next, pull and breathe as described earlier and shoot forward before kicking again. This approach teaches the independent movements of the arms and legs.

TO INCREASE DIFFICULTY

- Count to "three hippopotamus."

TO DECREASE DIFFICULTY

- Use a pull buoy far above your knees and kick.

Success Check

- You can perform the drill while maintaining a long body line.
- You do not move your hands and feet at the same time.

Score Your Success

1 point: You can go 10 yards.

3 points: You can go 25 yards.

5 points: You can go 25 yards in 10 or more pulls.

7 points: You can go 25 yards in 9 or fewer pulls.

Timing-and-Rhythm Drill 2   Two Kicks Per Stroke

This classic breaststroke drill increases your awareness of timing and body position; it also helps you with balance. It is performed by simply kicking twice in the stretched-out position with your hands far forward (but not on top of each other) and kicking twice per catch–pull sequence. Keep your head down with a long neck during each pair of kicks.

TO INCREASE DIFFICULTY

- Count to "three hippopotamus."

TO DECREASE DIFFICULTY

- Use a pull buoy far above your knees and kick.

Success Check

- You can perform the drill while maintaining a long body line.
- You do not move your hands and feet at the same time.

Score Your Success

1 point: You can go 10 yards.

3 points: You can go 25 yards.

5 points: You can go 25 yards in 10 or more pulls.

7 points: You can go 25 yards in 9 or fewer pulls.

Timing-and-Rhythm Drill 3
Breaststroke Pull With Dolphin Kick

This is another classic drill used by most modern breaststrokers. To do it, simply perform a breaststroke pull with one dolphin kick. (For the basic dolphin kick technique, see step 2.) This drill helps you with timing so that you can manipulate your center of buoyancy and ride the wave of propulsive force from your legs.

TO INCREASE DIFFICULTY

- Use only the pull while holding a pull buoy between your thighs.

TO DECREASE DIFFICULTY

- Use fins.

Success Check

- You can perform the drill while maintaining a long body line.
- You can move with an undulating rhythm.

Score Your Success

1 point: You can go 10 yards.

3 points: You can go 25 yards.

5 points: You can go 25 yards in 10 or more pulls.

7 points: You can go 25 yards in 9 or fewer pulls.

BREASTSTROKE PULLOUT

The modern breaststroke is done with what is referred to as a pullout (figure 5.4), both at the start and during each turn at the wall. To perform the pullout, the swimmer pushes off the wall underwater (or starts from a dive) in a streamlined position. As the hands separate, they can pull all the way down to the hips just once. The swimmer is allowed to perform one dolphin kick at any time in this part. As the swimmer slows, the hands are brought up the body and close to the body to get into a breast stroke swimming position with the hands out in front. It is at this point that the stroke as described earlier actually begins.

Figure 5.4 BREASTSTROKE PULLOUT

Preparation

1. While at the wall, place your feet about 1.5 to 2 feet (~0.5 m) underwater.
2. As you sink below the surface, touch your hands together in a streamlined position before pushing off of the wall forcefully.

Execution

1. You can dolphin-kick as you push off of the wall or at any time thereafter.
2. As your hands separate, wrap your fingers down toward the bottom of the pool in a circular motion and get your elbows up.
3. Push forcefully down to your thighs with both hands at the same time.
4. Sneak your hands back up along your body and out in front of your head.
5. Here, the first breaststroke kick happens, and you break the surface and begin the full stroke.

DRILL FOR BREASTSTROKE PULLOUT

Since this is the only stroke with a completely separate set of movements for getting into a swimming position, it is worth addressing the pullout separately with some stroke drills. The following drill allows you to practice conserving your momentum as you come off the wall. How you perform the pull—and for how long—depends on your fitness.

Pullout Drill   Multiple Pullouts

In this drill, you repeat the pullout motion underwater multiple times to gauge the timing.

TO INCREASE DIFFICULTY

- See how fast you can travel 25 yards.

TO DECREASE DIFFICULTY

- Do one pullout slowly and see how far you can go.

Success Check

- You can perform the drill while maintaining a long body line.
- You are not breaking the surface or too deep after the first pullout.

Score Your Success

1 point: You can go 10 yards.

3 points: You can go 25 yards.

5 points: You can go 25 yards in six or more pullouts.

7 points: You can go 25 yards in five or fewer pullouts.

SUCCESS SUMMARY

The breaststroke is unique in that about half of its propulsion derives from the kick and the rest derives from the pull. As a result, the stroke is highly rhythmic, and in order to do it well you need the lower half of your body to work independently of the upper half. This dynamic involves give and take, and there are many effective styles of breaststroke. One thing, however, is true for them all: If your timing is off, you spend a lot of energy going very slowly—or going nowhere fast.

SCORE YOUR SUCCESS

If you scored at least 32 points, then you have completed this step. If you scored 33 to 48 points, then you are well on your way and have the potential to develop your swimming stroke even further. If you scored more than 48 points, then you have mastered the key elements for taking your swimming to the next level.

Kicking Drills

1. Wall Kick   ___ out of 5
2. Moving Through the Water   ___ out of 7
3. Kicking on Your Front   ___ out of 7

Pulling Drills

1. Breaststroke Pull With Freestyle Kick   ___ out of 7
2. Tennis Ball or Fist   ___ out of 7

Breathing Drills

1. Tennis Ball 2   ___ out of 7

Timing-and-Rhythm Drills

1. Two-Hippopotamus Breaststroke   ___ out of 7
2. Two Kicks Per Stroke   ___ out of 7
3. Breaststroke Pull With Dolphin Kick   ___ out of 7

Pullout Drill

1. Multiple Pullouts   ___ out of 7
   Total   **___ out of 68**

Butterfly

The butterfly is the fourth of the competitive strokes recognized in international competition. It was developed in the 1930s as a way to minimize the drag caused by underwater recovery of the arms in the breaststroke. Early variants of the butterfly (referred to as the butterfly breaststroke) used an over-the-water recovery with a breaststroke kick. This technique was much faster than the breaststroke but required a great deal of strength. It was not until the 1950s that the butterfly was considered a separate stroke from breaststroke, and the use of a dolphin kick was added to the official competition rules governing the new stroke.

As mentioned in step 5, the butterfly, like the breaststroke, is considered a "short-axis" stroke but is really a timing-and-rhythm stroke. It does involve rotating on a shorter axis (i.e., through the chest, laterally) rather than on a long axis (down the spine), but the most important elements to keep in mind with this stroke are common to all of the strokes:

- Good body position
- Effective catch
- Pressure on the water throughout the stroke
- Acceleration throughout the stroke
- Kicking rhythm
- Effective breathing
- Effective timing

Once you have mastered all of these skills, you are well on your way to an effective butterfly.

The basic motion of the butterfly involves an undulating rhythm in which the legs and arms are synchronized by precise timing. The most important element of a good butterfly stroke is the use of the body's core, which is the greatest source of power.

Here are the basic movements as you flow through the stroke. From the neutral position described in step 1—facedown in the water with your arms stretched out above your head—press your chest down toward the pool bottom. To help you do so, you can use a downward motion of your feet with your legs together in a dolphin-kick downstroke.

Next, push your hips down while arching your back to bring your head and chest back toward the surface. Again, you are encouraged to use your legs in a dolphin-kick upstroke; you should feel some pressure on the backs of your legs and the bottoms of your feet. You use the dolphin kick here both to provide propulsive force and to manipulate the position of your center of buoyancy to produce an undulating motion.

As you complete the undulating and kicking motion, pitch your fingers down toward the bottom of the pool and bend at the elbows in a motion similar to that of pushing yourself up out of the pool. Once your hands and forearms are close to vertical, push back while accelerating your hands and arms. The propulsive force of your hands and forearms—along with a slight forward push of your chin—causes you to rise out of the water high enough to get a breath.

The last element involves acceleration of your hands past your hips and out of the water. With your head and shoulders out of the water, a forceful movement of your hands at the finish allows you to recover your arms in a straight fashion. The arms remain straight rather than bent over and parallel to the surface of the water. The entry of your hands and arms should be above your head in front of your shoulders, if not a little wider, thus returning you to your original neutral position to begin the next stroke cycle.

You will practice each of these elements in the following sections, which include drills to help you master each element and culminate in a discussion of putting it all together.

DOLPHIN KICK

Unlike the flutter kick, the dolphin kick derives its power from the middle part of your core—from the lower part of your rib cage down through your pelvis. In addition, your legs stay together the whole time. The basic motion involves driving your hips back and forth with the strong muscles of your core and using your legs merely to finish off the kick. Your legs should be long and loose; let your strong core muscles initiate most of the work.

A good mental image for this kick is the motion of a dolphin or whale. Try to mimic that motion with your body, from your chest on down. Some swimmers also find it helpful to imagine that their legs are glued together and cannot be separated.

In this step, you will work on the following skills:

1. Developing a propulsive and symmetrical kick
2. Laying your hands on the water and achieving a good catch position
3. Getting from the catch to the pull and making sure that the force is applied in the correct direction
4. Accelerating your hands through the pull
5. Synchronizing the kick and the pull
6. Effective breathing
7. Recovery of the arms

Dolphin Kick With Face Out of Water

The key here is to sustain a steady rhythmic kick (don't think about speed just yet) that feels like you are putting pressure on the water all the way down your leg. Remember to start the kick with your core and move fluidly down through your legs. Once you have mastered this motion (figure 6.1), it is time to move on to the next part of the progression.

Figure 6.1 **DOLPHIN KICK WITH FACE OUT OF WATER**

Preparation

1. The first part of the progression is to get in the water and grab the gutter.
2. From a standing position facing the wall, either kick or float your legs to the surface, making your body horizontal and parallel to the pool bottom.
3. At this stage, it is okay to use your forearms and the wall to help you achieve a horizontal position and to keep your head out of the water.
4. As you do this part, keep your legs as long and loose as possible (do not actively point your toes).
5. As your feet get to the surface, keep in mind that your goal is to put pressure on the water, which means that your legs must be *in* the water.

Execution

1. Keep your legs together and mimic the motion of a dolphin's tail.
2. This motion should be rhythmic and undulating rather than fast and jerky. You should feel the pressure on both the downstroke and the upstroke of the kick.

Dolphin Kick With Face in Water

In the first few parts of this progression, you have developed a mental image and achieved a horizontal position in the water while using your legs to maintain balance. The next part (figure 6.2) is to make sure that the kick you are developing is propulsive. Assume the same extended streamlined position that you developed in step 1. If your hands are grabbing the wall and hanging on instead of being pushed toward it, do a simple hands-to-toes check for correct positioning.

Figure 6.2 **DOLPHIN KICK WITH FACE IN WATER**

Preparation

1. The first part of this progression is to get in the water and grab the gutter.
2. From a standing position facing the wall, either kick or float your legs to the surface, making your body horizontal and parallel to the pool bottom.
3. At this stage, extend your arms all the way out.
4. As you do this part, keep your legs as long and loose as possible (do not actively point your toes).
5. As your feet get to the surface, remember that your goal is to put pressure on the water, which means that your legs must be *in* the water.

Execution

1. Once you are comfortable in the horizontal position, put your face in the water and extend your arms so that only your hands are on the wall.
2. As before, keep your legs together and mimic the motion of a dolphin's tail.
3. This motion should be rhythmic and undulating rather than fast and jerky. You should feel the pressure on both the downstroke and the upstroke of the kick.
4. You should feel yourself being pushed toward the wall on both the upstroke and the downstroke of the kick.

Dolphin Kick With Kickboard

Once again, this part (figure 6.3) of the progression ensures that your kick is indeed propulsive. If you come to a stop or even go backward, repeat the hands-to-toes check for correct positioning. Many swimmers come to the pool with a limited range of motion in their ankles. Make sure that your ankles are slightly plantar-flexed so that your toes point away from your body, but not so much as to make your legs rigid.

When you need to breathe, simply apply pressure to the kickboard and lift your head for air. Make this motion quick in order to maintain your balance in the water and get your face back in the water to stabilize your balance.

Figure 6.3 **DOLPHIN KICK WITH KICKBOARD**

Preparation

1. Using a kickboard for balance only, place your hands on the lower corners of the board.
2. Facing away from the wall in the water, pull your feet up, place them on the wall, and push off on your front.
3. Make sure that your face is in the water and look directly at the bottom of the pool.

Execution

1. Begin the same rhythmic kicking motion that you developed earlier in the progression; it should propel you down the pool at a very slow speed.

Dolphin Kick Without Kickboard

Once you have mastered the skill with the kickboard, it is time once again to put your propulsive kicking force to the test. Repeat the process just described, but this time do it without the assistance of the kickboard (figure 6.4). The goal is to kick in a streamlined position. If you were able to do so with a kickboard, then this transition should be a little easier. The new challenge here is that when you breathe, you should use the same sculling motion described earlier in step 2: Simply sweep your hands out and in rhythmically to apply enough pressure on the water to allow you to lift your head for a quick breath. Once you have mastered this technique—and it may take a few tries—it is time to move to dolphin kicking on your back.

Figure 6.4 DOLPHIN KICK WITHOUT KICKBOARD

Preparation

1. Facing away from the wall in the water, pull your feet up, place them on the wall, and push off on your front.
2. Make sure that your face is in the water and look directly at the bottom of the pool.

Execution

1. Begin the same rhythmic kicking motion that you developed earlier in the progression; it should propel you down the length of the pool at a very slow speed.
2. Sweep your hands out and in rhythmically to apply enough pressure on the water to allow you to lift your head for a quick breath.
3. Return your face to the water and continue.

Dolphin Kick on Your Back

Dolphin kicking on the back (figure 6.5) differs only slightly from kicking on the front. The upstroke of the kick is propulsive, whereas the downstroke is used to propel the arms in the recovery and entry. Once again, it is helpful to develop an effective mental image. As with kicking on your front, imagine the joints of each leg being connected by a rubber band; staying long and loose is still a key. This mental image helps you apply pressure in the right places and recruit the proper muscles.

Figure 6.5 **DOLPHIN KICK ON YOUR BACK**

Preparation

1. Make sure you have enough room to do the skill.
2. Facing the wall in the water, pull your feet up, place them on the wall, and push off on your back.

Execution

1. Begin the same rhythmic kicking motion that you developed earlier in the progression; it should propel you down the length of the pool at a very slow speed.
2. Maintain the streamline position.

MISSTEP

You can produce an effective wiggle but don't go anywhere.

CORRECTION

Remember that your hips initiate the kick. Begin by pushing your hips down, then your knees, and then your feet. Meanwhile, your upper body should remain in the same position.

MISSTEP

Your legs come apart during the kick.

CORRECTION

Imagine that your legs are glued together; squeeze your knees together and try not to overpower the kick. Keep everything fluid and dolphinlike.

DRILLS FOR DOLPHIN KICKING

Once you have mastered the basic movement, continue to develop your technique. Many swimmers start off stiff and mechanical in their kicking rhythm; with practice, however, they develop a smoother and much more propulsive kick. Here are a few drills to help you master this skill.

Dolphin Kicking Drill 1   Vertical Kicking

After you have achieved propulsion in dolphin kicking, work on kicking both up and down. This drill helps you develop a symmetrical kick. Find water deep enough to be over your head, then begin by treading water with your head out and using a flutter kick. Once you are comfortable, switch to a dolphin kick.

The goal here is to remain stationary in the water without making much use of your hands. If you kick more forcefully in one direction, you will drift around in the pool. Staying in place, on the other hand, means that you are putting pressure on the water with both the fronts and the backs of your legs. You should feel the pressure most on the tops and bottoms of your feet, since they are the body parts that finish off the kick.

TO INCREASE DIFFICULTY

- Do not use your hands at all for balance.
- Put your hands on top of your head.
- Raise your hands straight above you in a streamlined position.

TO DECREASE DIFFICULTY

- Use fins.
- Use a kickboard.

Success Check

- You can perform the drill without fins.
- You can feel pressure on the tops and bottoms of your feet.
- You stay stationary when doing vertical kicking.
- You feel your body lift slightly out of the water.

Score Your Success

1 point: You can do the drill with fins.

3 points: You can do the drill without fins for 20 seconds.

5 points: You can do the drill without fins for more than 25 seconds.

Once you have felt an effective propulsive force with the lower part of your body, it is time to start working on applying this force in a horizontal rather than a vertical direction.

Dolphin Kicking Drill 2   Kick on Your Back

This drill helps you continue to develop a symmetrical kick. Now that you feel the pressure on the water, it is time to ensure that it is propulsive pressure by moving through the water. The next part of the progression for an effective dolphin kick is to lie on your back in the neutral position described in step 1 with your hands at your sides for balance.

Begin dolphin-kicking with special emphasis on the pressure on the bottoms of your feet. As with the backstroke flutter kick, keep your knees underwater; do not just "push" at the water with the tops of your feet. Some swimmers find it beneficial to think of curling the toes in order to feel the feet in a stretched-out position while keeping the ankles loose.

Important note! You will not be able to see where you are going during this drill. Make sure that the backstroke flags are in place—5 yards from the wall—or have your coach or instructor stop you when necessary!

TO INCREASE DIFFICULTY

- Place a kickboard across the upper part of your legs to prevent your upper legs from coming out of the water.
- Raise your arms above your head and perform the drill in a streamlined position.

TO DECREASE DIFFICULTY

- Use two kickboards—one in each hand—for balance.
- Use a slight sculling motion to provide a little propulsion at the same time.
- Use fins.

(continued)

Dolphin Kicking Drill 2 *(continued)*

Success Check

- You can kick for 25 yards on your back using your hands for balance.
- You can go 25 yards with ease on your back in a streamlined position.

Score Your Success

1 point: You can go 10 yards.

3 points: You can go 25 yards.

5 points: You can go 25 yards in 15 or more kicks.

7 points: You can go 25 yards in fewer than 15 kicks.

Dolphin Kicking Drill 3   Kick on Your Front

The next drill for constructing an effective dolphin kick involves transferring the back kick from the neutral position to the front. Squeeze your ankles together and point your toes while finishing the kick. Do this drill first with your hands at your sides for balance, then switch to a streamlined position. Repeat the same motion until you are comfortable with it.

TO INCREASE DIFFICULTY

- Stay in a streamlined position.

TO DECREASE DIFFICULTY

- Use a kickboard out front or even lie on it.
- Use a slight sculling motion to provide a little propulsion at the same time.
- Use fins.

Success Check

- You can kick for 25 yards on your front with a board and fins.
- You can kick for 25 yards on your front with a board and without fins.
- You can go 25 yards with ease on your front without a kickboard and without fins.

Score Your Success

1 point: You can go 10 yards.

3 points: You can go 25 yards.

5 points: You can go 25 yards in less than 30 seconds.

7 points: You can go 50 yards in less than 60 seconds.

BUTTERFLY ARMSTROKE

Since its inception, the butterfly armstroke (figure 6.6) has been taught in many ways. In the early years, many instructors advocated an outsweep of the hands and a movement in a keyhole fashion. Later variants included an insweep, as well making almost a figure-eight pattern. The modern butterfly uses more of a straight pull with the maximum amount of arm area perpendicular to the direction in which you are going.

Figure 6.6   **BUTTERFLY ARMSTROKE**

Preparation

1. At the end of the pool, lie on the water in the facedown neutral position.
2. Your hands should be shoulder-width apart or slightly wider, depending on your entry or initial stroke.

Execution

1. Flex your wrists and point your fingers down toward the bottom of the pool.
2. As you do so, your elbows rotate out and bend, creating a good catch and getting much of the surface area of your hands and forearms close to vertical and thus perpendicular to the direction in which you want to go.
3. The pull is straight back, and the pitch of your hands changes to keep them vertical for longer during the stroke.
4. Finish by accelerating your hands through the end of the stroke.

DRILLS FOR BUTTERFLY ARM MOVEMENT

When you watch accomplished butterfly swimmers, you see the recovery, but the real magic happens underwater. That is where the positioning of the hands, elbows, forearms, and shoulders really comes into play. When doing the following drills, remember that you are not pushing down but pulling forward.

Butterfly Arm Movement Drill 1   Wall Press

This drill teaches you the correct catch and pull through the armstroke. To perform the drill, get in the pool in water that is over your head. Place your hands at least shoulder-width apart on the pool deck and submerge until your arms are fully extended. Once you have achieved this position, apply pressure to your hands and pull yourself toward the surface. Once at the surface, continue the motion until you are halfway out of the water with your arms extended to your hips. Repeat this drill until you can do it with your eyes closed.

TO INCREASE DIFFICULTY

- Start at the bottom of the pool, extend your arms up, and place them on the deck after they break the surface.

TO DECREASE DIFFICULTY

- Use fins for extra lift.
- Start in shallow water and push off of the bottom to get extra lift.

Success Check

- You can press all the way up with no assistance.
- You can start on the bottom, place your hands on the deck, and press all the way up.

Score Your Success

1 point: You can perform the drill in shallow water.

3 points: You can perform the drill in deep water with fins.

5 points: You can perform the drill five times in deep water without fins.

7 points: You can perform the drill from the bottom in deep water five times or more.

Butterfly Arm Movement Drill 2   Sneaky Hands

This drill allows you to focus only on the catch and pull. Begin by lying on the water facedown in the neutral position with your legs together and your arms extended over your head. Separate each motion into a distinct movement as you pitch your fingers down, rotate your elbows up, and push through to finish with your hands past your hips. Accelerate your hands through the entire movement.

Once you have completed the movement, your hands are at your thighs and you are moving forward. Now, sneak your hands back up along your body, keeping your elbows in until you are at the first position, then repeat. This is very similar to the breaststroke pullout.

TO INCREASE DIFFICULTY

- Once you are comfortable with this drill, add one dolphin kick prior to moving your hands back and another after finishing the pull at your thighs.

TO DECREASE DIFFICULTY

- Use a snorkel so that you can leave your face in the water.
- Stop after each cycle to reset.

Success Check

- You can feel the water on your hands and forearms.
- You can go 25 yards with ease on your front in nine or fewer pulls.

Score Your Success

1 point: You can go 10 yards.

3 points: You can go 25 yards.

5 points: You can go 25 yards in 10 or more pulls.

7 points: You can go 25 yards in fewer than 10 pulls with the kicks.

BUTTERFLY ARM RECOVERY

Many swimmers struggle with arm recovery (figure 6.7) if they perform the pull incorrectly. It is easy for the arms to recover over the water if the hands accelerate through the stroke and finish at or slightly wider than the hips. The reason is that the momentum of the stroke carries the hands through the exit, which means that less effort is required to bring the arms and hands back to the forward position.

The key is to finish the stroke fast and feather the hands so that they exit the water smoothly, pinkies out first. If the stroke is finished with an acceleration, the forward movement of the arms requires less effort. It should be done in the same position: little fingers up, thumbs down, and forearms and upper arms parallel to the water. The specifics of how the hands enter the water are matters of style. Some swimmers do it thumb first, whereas others rotate the wrists before entry. Regardless of style, one must ensure that the fingers are down as described in the catch-and-pull phase. Therefore, if you use the thumbs-first option, make sure to rotate your fingers and hands to be perpendicular to the direction in which you are traveling.

Figure 6.7 **BUTTERFLY ARM RECOVERY**

Preparation

1. Lie facedown on the water, as described for the preceding skills and drills, with your hands shoulder-width or a little farther apart.
2. Make sure that you have plenty of room down the lane to perform the skill.

Execution

1. Pull forward as described in the previous section on the wall press.
2. Pay careful attention to accelerating your hands through the pull phase.
3. Sweep your hands past your thighs and let them breach the surface of the water as if to throw them forward.
4. As your hands exit the water, your pinkies should be up and your thumbs down, thus allowing for a clean release from the water.
5. If finished with an acceleration, the forward movement of the arms requires less effort; it should be done in the same position.
6. Perform the entry by laying your hands on the water rather than slapping them into it.
7. Your hands should enter shoulder-width apart if not a little wider.

DRILLS FOR BUTTERFLY ARM RECOVERY

The most important part of the recovery is to accelerate your hands at the finish of the stroke. If this movement is done with great force, your hands and arms will recover almost by themselves. If you find yourself struggling to get your hands out of the water, check your positioning and practice the following drills.

Butterfly Arm Recovery Drill 1   Dolphin Dive

This classic drill helps you get used to the undulating motion and provides buoyant force support while you coordinate the over-the-water recovery. To perform it, stand in waist-deep water with your hands at your sides, then bend at the waist so that your chest is in the water but your shoulders are out. Your chin should touch the water as you look at a spot 8 to 10 inches (20-25 cm) in front of your face.

Next, rotate your hands—so that your pinkies are up and your thumbs down—and sweep them forward over the water; near the beginning of the movement, put your face in the water. Now place your hands in the water in front of your shoulders or slightly wider. Push yourself forward off of the bottom and stretch out on the water while pushing your chest and your hips down toward the bottom. This is the same kicking motion described earlier. Pull yourself forward and, when your hands reach your hips, stop and stand up. Repeating this drill causes an undulating motion that serves as the basis for your stroke and allows you time to isolate the recovery portion of the stroke.

TO INCREASE DIFFICULTY

• Decrease the time between repetitions.

TO DECREASE DIFFICULTY

• Use a snorkel so that you can leave your face in the water.
• Stop after each cycle to reset.
• Use fins.

Success Check

• You can feel the undulating rhythm.
• Your arms stay parallel to the water on the recovery.
• You can go 25 yards with few or no pauses between cycles.

Score Your Success

1 point: You can go 10 yards.

3 points: You can go 25 yards.

5 points: You can go 25 yards in 10 or more pulls.

7 points: You can go 25 yards in fewer than 10 pulls with the kicks.

Butterfly Arm Recovery Drill 2   Arm Sweep

This drill incorporates the motions of kicking and pulling without the over-the-water recovery. As in the Sneaky Hands drill, you perform all elements of the stroke, except that when you finish the stroke you sweep your hands and arms forward and out to the sides, near the surface of the water but still in it.

Start with your hands and arms extended out front and lie on the water in the neutral position. Do a dolphin kick, both up and down, as well as a catch and pull. As you finish the pull, sweep your hands and arms out in a semicircular motion with your arms straight. It is okay for your arms to skim the surface of the water. When your hands reach the front, stop and stand up to reset the stroke. When performing this drill, keep your arms straight and lead with your thumbs while in the water. This technique helps with body positioning so you do not get the body too vertical.

TO INCREASE DIFFICULTY

- Once you are comfortable with this drill, add one dolphin kick prior to moving your hands back and another one after finishing the pull at your thighs.
- Breathe by sculling in the front rather than stopping and touching the bottom.

TO DECREASE DIFFICULTY

- Use a snorkel so that you can leave your face in the water.
- Stop after each cycle to reset.
- Use fins.

Success Check

- You can feel the undulating rhythm.
- Your arms stay straight in the water on the recovery.
- You can go 25 yards with few or no pauses between cycles.

Score Your Success

1 point: You can go 10 yards.

3 points: You can go 25 yards.

5 points: You can go 25 yards in 10 or more pulls.

7 points: You can go 25 yards in fewer than 10 pulls with the kicks.

BREATHING

The timing of the breath is critical to a good butterfly stroke. As with the breast-stroke, breathing at the wrong time during the butterfly stroke cycle not only slows the stroke but also increases the rate of fatigue. However, whereas mistimed breathing in the breaststroke mainly makes you slow, mistimed breathing in the butterfly exhausts you and forces you to stop.

To learn when to breathe and how to do so with proper technique, you use a few simple mental cues and drills (figure 6.8). The first cue addresses how high to rise out of the water when getting air. Rising too high reduces momentum and undulation. As a corrective, think of pushing your chin forward rather than lifting your head.

The next concern is the timing of your breathing. Many swimmers breathe late. To avoid this pitfall, initiate the forward chin movement as you start your pull and make it a quick breath. How often you breathe depends on your individual needs and development as a swimmer. Conventional wisdom used to recommend breathing on every other stroke and leaving your face in the water rather than getting air on each stroke. However, after several Olympians chose to breathe either on every stroke or in a one-two pattern, it became apparent that butterfly swimmers should breathe as often as they need to—but not more.

Figure 6.8 **BUTTERFLY BREATHING**

Preparation

1. Review the preceding skill discussions of arm stroking, recovery, and positioning.
2. Start at the end of the pool and make sure that you have plenty of room to perform the skill.

Execution

1. As you begin to pull back—with your fingers down and your elbows up, as described in previous skills—push your chin slightly forward.
2. The change of position and the flow of water against your chest allow your mouth and nose to be right at the surface of the water in order to get air.
3. Exhale while your face is in the water so that you can get quick air while your face is out.
4. Make sure that your face returns to the water as your hands exit on the recovery.

MISSTEP

Many swimmers lift the head and then drop it back down, almost as if nodding or bobbing for apples. The problem here is that when the head goes up, the hips sink.

CORRECTION

Remember not to lift your head but instead to push your chin forward. The flow of water against your chest will give you some lift.

MISSTEP

You breath too late, and your hips sink.

CORRECTION

Initiate your breathing as soon as you start the pull. Your face should go back into the water as your arms recover. If you see your hands, it is too late.

Butterfly Breathing Drill   Dolphin-Dive Sneak-a-Breath

This drill involves lying on the water and performing a catch and pull along with the kicking motion from the first drills. As you start the pull, push your chin forward to get air. With your hands still at your thighs, place your face back in the water and sneak your hands forward beneath you.

TO INCREASE DIFFICULTY

• Speed up the rhythm.

TO DECREASE DIFFICULTY

• Use fins.
• Stop after each cycle to reset.

Success Check

• You get your face back in the water before moving your hands forward.
• You pull forward instead of pressing down to get air.
• You can go 25 yards on your front in nine or fewer pulls with ease.

Score Your Success

1 point: You can go 10 yards.

3 points: You can go 25 yards.

5 points: You can go 25 yards in 10 or more pulls.

7 points: You can go 25 yards in fewer than 10 pulls with the kicks.

TIMING AND RHYTHM

Timing is crucial in both the breaststroke and the butterfly, but especially in the butterfly; if your timing is off, you go slow and wear out fast. Here is a brief review of how the butterfly rhythm works (discussed earlier at the beginning of this step).

From the neutral position, push your chest down and your hips up while kicking down, then push your hips down and your chest up while kicking up. Position your fingers down and your elbows up while pushing your chin forward. Pull through and accelerate your hands while coming up for air. Flip your hands and arms out, down past your hips, and around in a sweeping motion while also placing your face back in the water and kicking down again.

DRILLS FOR TIMING AND RHYTHM

Here are a few simple drills that you can do to emphasize timing.

Timing-and-Rhythm Drill 1   1-2-3-4-5 Butterfly

This drill separates the propulsive movements. Perform each distinct movement described in the summary of butterfly rhythm, waiting one or two seconds between movements. As you get more comfortable with the movements and with the timing, reduce the wait interval until you are swimming the full-stroke butterfly. Breathe on every stroke if necessary and less often if possible.

To do the drill, lie facedown on the water in the neutral position with your hands in front. Then implement the five elements referred to in the numbers of the drill name (1-2-3-4-5 Butterfly): (1) push your chest down, (2) push your hips down and your chest up, (3) pitch your fingers down, (4) pull through, and (5) recover. The idea here is to slow the movements into separate and distinct actions. You can speed up as you become more comfortable with the rhythm.

TO INCREASE DIFFICULTY
- Speed up the rhythm.

TO DECREASE DIFFICULTY
- Use fins.
- Stop after each cycle to reset.
- Use a snorkel.

Success Check
- You get your face back in the water before moving your hands forward.
- You pull forward instead of pressing down to get air.
- You can go 25 yards with ease on your front in 10 or fewer pulls.
- You don't need fins.
- You can establish a breathing pattern right away.

Score Your Success

1 point: You can go 10 yards.

3 points: You can go 25 yards.

5 points: You can go 25 yards in 10 or more pulls.

7 points: You can go 25 yards in 9 or fewer pulls.

Timing-and-Rhythm Drill 2   Four Kicks Per Stroke

This drill is designed to help you optimize your hand entry and maintain a good line of the body in the water. To do it, perform one pull for every four dolphin kicks. This technique isolates your hand positioning upon entry and immediately afterward. Lay your hands on the water directly in front of you so that your arms are above the head in an outstretched position like that of Superman when flying. Perform four dolphin kicks to continue moving forward while adjusting your hands and arms if necessary.

If you find yourself having to lift your head and pitch your hands up to get back to the stretched-out position, you are driving the stroke too much with your upper body. Instead, think of laying your hands on the water and landing on your armpits. Remember to breathe only in the beginning part of the stroke.

TO INCREASE DIFFICULTY

- Speed up the rhythm.

TO DECREASE DIFFICULTY

- Use fins.
- Stop after each cycle to reset.
- Use a snorkel.

Success Check

- You get your face back in the water before moving your hands forward.
- You pull forward instead of pressing down to get air.
- You can go 25 yards on your front in 10 or fewer pulls with ease.
- You don't need fins.
- You can establish a breathing pattern right away.

Score Your Success

1 point: You can go 10 yards.

3 points: You can go 25 yards.

5 points: You can go 25 yards in 10 or more pulls.

7 points: You can go 25 yards in 9 or fewer pulls.

Timing-and-Rhythm Drill 3   3-3-3

This drill comes in several versions. One of the most effective approaches goes as follows: Do three strokes with only your right arm while your left arm is out front; do three strokes with only your left arm while your right arm is out front; and then swim three full strokeswith both arms together. The timing of the drill is key.

Unlike the freestyle one-arm, this drill requires you to remain flat; that is, your hips must stay flat rather than rotating from side to side. Use your extended (nonstroking) arm for balance. Also be sure to breathe to your front, not to your side as you would in freestyle.

TO INCREASE DIFFICULTY

- Increase the pace.
- Breathe on every stroke.

TO DECREASE DIFFICULTY

- Use fins to prevent that stalling feeling and to isolate the catch and pull and the timing of your breathing. Make sure that your face is back in the water before you initiate the catch.
- Use a snorkel.

Success Check

- You can remain flatter on the water.
- You can complete the drill with one arm without twisting.
- You can get through three full strokes without struggling.

Score Your Success

1 point: You can do it with fins.

2 points: You can do it with fins and your hands are in front before your face is back in the water.

3 points: You can do the drill for a few strokes.

4 points: You can do the drill for 25 yards.

5–10 points: You can do the drill more than 30 yards (5 points) and perhaps up to 50 yards (10 points).

Turns

You need to be able to perform an effective turn in both competitive and recreational pool swimming. In competition, an effective turn saves race time when changing direction. For recreational and fitness swimmers, an effective turn maximizes your workout time and enhances your proficiency in the water. Every turn, regardless of the type, consists of four key elements:

1. Approach
2. Exchange
3. Streamline
4. Breakout

The approach involves where, when, and how you prepare for the turn. The exchange is the point at which you transfer momentum from one direction to the opposite direction. The streamline is performed when you push off of the wall, and the breakout is where you transition from streamlining to swimming a stroke. In this step, you learn how to perform the most basic turn for recreational swimming, as well as the most advanced turns and transitions used in competitive swimming.

OPEN TURN

The most basic and functional turn is the open turn. It was used in early freestyle competitions, as well as backstroke competitions, and is a favorite among recreational swimmers. In this turn, the approach (figure 7.1) is made on the front, and in competition pools it can be gauged by markings on the pool bottom. Specifically, the centerline of each lane has a T shape close to the wall that provides competitive swimmers with a target. When swimming in a pool without this kind of marking, you can take a quick look to judge distance by lifting your head out of the water. Many pools also have a spillover gutter system or a low coping that allows you to grasp the wall with your hands.

Figure 7.1 **OPEN TURN PHASE 1: APPROACH AND EXCHANGE**

Preparation

1. As you approach the wall, take a final stroke, leave one hand at your thigh (pointed in the direction opposite of the wall), extend your other arm toward the wall, and roll onto your side.

Execution

1. As your momentum carries you into the wall, grasp the wall (or push away from it with your hand) while driving your knees up toward your chest.

2. During the exchange, your body rotates. As you let go of the wall, place your feet on the wall about shoulder-width apart.

3. Your trailing arm should still be pointed down the pool underwater.

4. The arm that just let go of the wall should come over your head and meet your other hand in the water while you are still on your side.

5. At this point, your feet should be planted on the wall, your knees bent at about 90 degrees, and your hands together over your head in a streamlined position pointed down the pool.

MISSTEP

You come to a stop before you reach the wall, or you end up with your face very close to the wall or hit the wall with your arm.

CORRECTION

Take one more stroke, or one fewer, to adjust your distance.

The next phase of the turn involves the push-off and streamline (figure 7.2). This is a critical part of good swimming; in fact, other than a start or dive, this is the fastest that you can move the in water without some sort of aid. As in step 1, the push-off here should be forceful; in addition, since you are on your side, you need to rotate to the correct position during the streamline. Make sure that you are underwater and parallel to the pool bottom and the surface of the water.

Another key here lies in the fact that your head position controls your depth on the streamline. If you keep your chin and head down, you maintain constant depth. If you lift your head or push your chin forward, you rise toward the surface. Experiment with how long your streamline should be for best results.

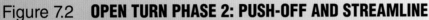

Figure 7.2 **OPEN TURN PHASE 2: PUSH-OFF AND STREAMLINE**

Preparation

1. Once you have completed the approach and gotten your feet on the wall, it is time for the exchange.
2. Get your last air prior to executing the rest of the turn.
3. While you are still on your side, bring the hand that just let go of the wall over your head to meet your other hand in the water.

Execution

1. Make sure that your hands touch; your body sinks to the level of your feet.
2. The push is critical for getting a good streamline, so push off forcefully.
3. As soon as you push off, begin kicking rhythmically; do not wait to slow down.

MISSTEP

You push off of the wall but are not underwater.

CORRECTION

As your hand leaves the wall, move it over your head to meet your other hand underwater. Delay the push until you sink to the level of your feet.

The last part of the turn is the breakout (figure 7.3), which is your transition from the streamlined position to a swimming position. In freestyle swimming, simply push your chin forward. Please note that you should not necessarily lift your head; instead, bring your chin forward, which causes you to rise to the surface gradually. In contrast, lifting your head causes you to become more vertical, thus losing momentum and slowing down.

Figure 7.3 OPEN TURN PHASE 3: BREAKOUT

Preparation

1. Complete all previous parts of the progression, then push off forcefully.
2. As you push off, make sure that you are streamlined.
3. Begin kicking as described earlier.

Execution

1. Push your chin forward.
2. Forcefully take a first stroke.
3. Your head, shoulders, and hips should all break the surface at about the same time.

MISSTEP
You turn over and face the direction in which you want to go.

CORRECTION
If you are on your side, you should face one of the sides of the pool rather than looking down the lane. Make sure that you are on your side.

OPEN TURN FOR BACKSTROKE

You can also use an open turn with the backstroke, even in competition (figure 7.4). For safety reasons, you should practice this technique *only* in a pool equipped with backstroke flags. As mentioned in the backstroke step, these are placed 5 yards from the end of the pool. Swimmers also count strokes from the flags to get to the wall, and for many swimmers it takes about three strokes.

As you approach on your back, roll toward your side, as in freestyle. Make sure not to go past vertical with your shoulders; that is, remain slightly on your back. The exchange is the same as in freestyle, and the streamline is similar except that you push off slightly on your back. The streamline is faceup, and the breakout is the same as before except this time of course transitioning into the backstroke.

Figure 7.4 OPEN TURN FOR BACKSTROKE

Preparation

1. When approaching on your back, roll toward your side. Do not go past vertical with your shoulders; instead, remain slightly on your back.
2. Push off slightly on your back.
3. The streamline is faceup.

Execution

1. Many backstrokers benefit from using a powerful underwater dolphin kick to maintain momentum.
2. Since you are on your back, it is helpful to use a nose clip or breathe out slowly through your nose.
3. Touching chin to the chest; your chin helps you rise to the surface.
4. As you break the surface, rotate slightly toward the arm with which you will pull first.
5. Take the first few strokes with great power as you transition to a flutter kick.

MISSTEP

You push off and immediately go to either the bottom or the top of the water.

CORRECTION

Make sure that your feet are planted and in line with your hips and shoulders to produce a powerful push in the right direction.

MISSTEP

You push off on top of the water without ever submerging.

CORRECTION

Be patient while your feet are on the wall. As your arm goes over, breathe out slightly while on your side or back in order to sink before pushing.

DRILLS FOR OPEN TURNS

The open turn is a great turn to learn first because it is often used by fitness swimmers. In addition, until the 1960s, it was used by distance swimmers in competition to get more oxygen during turns. The following drills help you master the elements of the turn.

Open Turn Drill 1   Approach

To perform this drill, get in water that is about 3 to 4 feet (1 m) deep. Position yourself two or three yards away from the wall and start by pushing off of the bottom in a streamlined position. Take one freestyle stroke, rotate to your nonstroking side, and reach for the wall. Let your momentum carry you and attend closely to the pool markings. Grab the gutter or coping and pull yourself forward slightly. Try both sides—you will find one more comfortable and easier than the other. Adjust your distance from the wall as needed.

TO INCREASE DIFFICULTY

• Start farther from the wall and take multiple strokes prior to the touch and grab.

TO DECREASE DIFFICULTY

• Start closer to the wall and just push off and glide on one side without taking a stroke.

Success Check

- You are laid out on your side with one hand out and the other at your side.
- Your top shoulder and hip are at the surface of the water.
- Your head is laid out on your extended arm.

1 point: You can do the drill using just the push-off.

3 points: You can do the drill with one stroke.

5 points: You can do the drill from farther out and take multiple strokes.

Open Turn Drill 2   Exchange

Once you have mastered drill 1, it is time to work on the exchange. Stand in water that is about 3 to 4 feet (1 m) deep and position yourself about one arm's length from the side of the pool. If the pool's design permits, grab the gutter with either hand and turn sideways so that your side, rather than your front, faces the wall. If you can't grab the gutter, grab the coping or deck. Point your other arm down the length of the pool underwater. Drive your knees toward your chest and rotate your feet to the wall about 2 to 3 feet (0.6 to 0.9 m) underwater. You are now on your side and tucked, with your feet on the wall and one arm pointing down the length of the pool. Sink and touch your hands together so that you are on your side underwater. Do not push; the idea here is to get comfortable in the proper position for pushing effectively.

TO INCREASE DIFFICULTY

- Make sure that your hand leaves the wall before your feet touch, then hold the wall position for three to five seconds.
- Raise your hands straight above you in a streamlined position.

TO DECREASE DIFFICULTY

- Keep your hand on the wall.

Success Check

- You can perform the drill without floating away from the wall.
- Your feet, hips, and shoulders are all at the same level in the water when you sink.
- You are in a streamlined position from the waist up.

1 point: You can do the drill with one hand keeping you on the wall.

3 points: You can do the drill without a hand on the wall.

5 points: You can do the drill and hold the position for three to five seconds.

Open Turn Drill 3   Side-to-Front Streamline

Once you have mastered drill 2, it is time to work on the streamline and push. This drill is performed in three stages. In the first stage, push off of the wall in a streamlined position with your head down to control depth. The key is to push off forcefully and go as far as you can. Find markers in the pool or use another means to determine where you come up each time. This is only a push and a streamline—no kicking or other movements. In the second stage, glide as far as you can. In the third, rotate from the side to the front while gliding and using only body control. Since you are on your side for the open turn, practice rotating from the side to the front several times. Do the same for the backstroke (rotating to the back).

TO INCREASE DIFFICULTY

- Combine this drill with the approach and exchange drills.

TO DECREASE DIFFICULTY

- Just sink to the streamlined position in any way you prefer and push.

Success Check

- You are in a streamlined position before you push.
- You can go at least to the flags—that is, 5 yards—with no body movement before surfacing.

Score Your Success

1 point: You can go 5 yards.

3 points: You can go 7 yards.

5 points: You can go 10 yards.

7 points: You can go 12 yards.

Open Turn Drill 4   1-2-3 Streamlines

This drill is also performed in three phases. The first phase is the push, and the second is the kicking. These phases are closely linked; there should be little or no gliding prior to getting into your kicking rhythm. The third phase involves pushing your chin forward to initiate the breakout. Each of these three elements constitutes a separate skill that must be put in place with good timing. Use trial and error to determine how many kicks to perform and when to break the surface. Practice this drill on both your front and your back, using both the flutter kick and the dolphin kick.

TO INCREASE DIFFICULTY

- Combine this drill with the approach and exchange drills.

TO DECREASE DIFFICULTY

- Just sink to the streamlined position in any way you prefer, then push and kick.

Success Check

- You are in a streamlined position before you push.
- You can go at least to the flags or 5 yards before surfacing.
- You can do the drill with both flutter and dolphin kicks.

Score Your Success

1 point: You can go 5 yards.

3 points: You can go 7 yards.

5 points: You can go 10 yards.

7 points: You can go 12 yards.

Open Turn Drill 5   Three-Stroke Spin

The purpose of this drill is to maintain the momentum that you generate by pushing off of the wall. After you have done the drills listed already and mastered them, it is time to finish the turn, which means transitioning from streamlining to swimming. This drill is performed by pushing off and getting into a kicking rhythm, then pushing your chin forward to rise to the surface and taking three fast strokes—almost like spinning your arms. Many swimmers lose momentum during the breakout, and it is important to maintain as much velocity as you can. Practice this drill with varying streamline lengths. Stop after just three strokes. Try it for both freestyle and backstroke using both flutter and dolphin kicks.

TO INCREASE DIFFICULTY

- Take three or more strokes before your first breath.

TO DECREASE DIFFICULTY

- Shorten your streamline and breakout to get air sooner.

Success Check

- You are in a streamlined position before you push.
- You can go at least to the flags—that is, 5 yards—before surfacing.
- You can do the drill with both flutter and dolphin kicks.
- You can get halfway down the pool—that is, 12.5 yards—with three strokes.

Score Your Success

1 point: You can go 5 yards.

3 points: You can go 7 yards.

5 points: You can go 10 yards.

7 points: You can go 12 yards.

TWO-HAND TOUCH TURN

The two-hand touch turn is the one used in competition and recreational swimming for both the breaststroke and the butterfly. To perform this turn, the approach (figure 7.5) is made on the front, and in competition pools it can be gauged by markings on the pool bottom. Specifically, the centerline of each lane has a T shape close to the wall that provides competitive swimmers with a target. Since both the breaststroke and the butterfly are forward-looking strokes, you can also easily sneak a peek at your distance from the wall. Many pools also have a spillover gutter system or a low coping that allows you to grasp the wall with your hands. This technique reduces your length and thus the resistance during your turn and causes your feet to come up close to the wall for the exchange.

Figure 7.5 **TWO-HAND TOUCH TURN: APPROACH**

Preparation

1. As you approach the wall, take a final stroke and reach for the wall with both hands.
2. Stretch for the wall rather than taking an additional short stroke.

Execution

1. As your momentum carries you into the wall, grasp it (or push away from it with your hands).
2. Drive your knees up toward your chest.
3. Rotate your feet toward the wall.

MISSTEP
You come to a stop before reaching the wall, or you end up with your face very close to the wall or hit the wall with your arm.

CORRECTION
Take one more stroke, or one fewer, to adjust your distance.

MISSTEP
You have to take a half-stroke because you are too close.

CORRECTION
It is better to be long on the turn than short. In breaststroke competition, the drag is increased and slows you down, and the pull must also be followed by a kick, according to current rules. This could lead to a disqualification, so it is preferable to glide to the wall.

During the exchange (figure 7.6), your body rotates and you draw one arm back toward the other end of the pool and then extend your hand. This motion causes your body to transition from being breast-down to being on your side. As in the open turn, as you rotate your feet to the wall, your other hand goes over your head and meets the first hand underwater to complete this part of the turn.

Figure 7.6   **TWO-HAND TOUCH TURN: EXCHANGE**

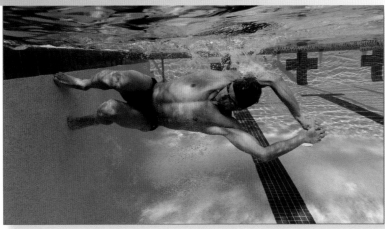

Preparation

1. Approach the wall as described.

Execution

1. Once your body rotates, draw one of your arms back toward the other end of the pool and then extend your hand.

2. As in the open turn, as you rotate your feet to the wall, your other hand goes over your head and meets the first hand underwater.

3. Make sure to get your last breath before your hands touch underwater.

MISSTEP

You turn over and face the direction in which you want to go.

CORRECTION

Turn your face to the ceiling or sky to get a little extra air and ensure that you don't twist on the wall. Make sure that you are on your side when you push.

The next phase of the turn involves the push-off and streamline (figure 7.7). As in step 1, the push-off here should be forceful; in addition, since you are on your side, you need to rotate to the correct position during the streamline. Also as before, your head position controls your depth on the streamline.

Figure 7.7   **TWO-HAND TOUCH TURN: PUSH-OFF AND STREAMLINE**

Preparation

1. Complete the previous two skills.
2. Position yourself on your side in a near-streamlined position with your feet on the wall.

Execution

1. Make sure that your hands touch each other; your body sinks to the level of your feet.
2. The push is critical for getting a good streamline. So push off forcefully.
3. Rotate to the correct position during the streamline.
4. As soon as you push off, begin kicking rhythmically; do not wait to slow down.

MISSTEP

You rotate on the wall and are facedown.

CORRECTION

Draw your knees up while twisting only slightly so that you are on your side when you are ready to push.

The last part of the turn is the breakout (figure 7.8), in which you transition from the streamlined position to a swimming position. For the butterfly and breaststroke, the first movement is the kick, so you will need to be near the surface. To get there, simply push your chin forward. Please note that you should not necessarily lift your head; instead, bring your chin forward, which causes you to rise to the surface gradually. As in all of these breakouts, make sure to be neither too shallow nor too deep.

Figure 7.8 **TWO-HAND TOUCH TURN: BREAKOUT**

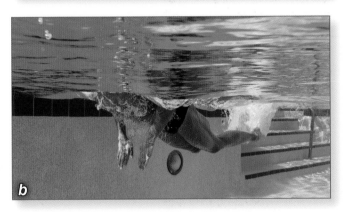

Preparation

1. Push off in a streamline.

Execution

1. Get near the surface and push your chin forward.
2. As you break the surface, take a forceful first stroke.
3. Initiate the dolphin kick immediately off of the wall and sweep your hands out to the catch position on the breakout.

MISSTEP
You break out too deep and then have to rise fast to get air.

CORRECTION
Remember that your head position controls your depth. As you push your chin forward, you will rise to the surface.

DRILLS FOR TWO-HAND TOUCH TURN

Concentrate on each movement separately in order to master them and build a highly effective turn. The key is to get on and off of the wall quickly with no energy wasted. With this goal in mind, the best turners avoid having their feet and their hands on the wall at the same time. Work toward that goal as you practice the following drills.

Two-Hand Touch-Turn Drill 1   Approach

Both the breaststroke and the butterfly are based on good timing and rhythm, and this holds true for the turn. One of the ways to practice being ready for the turn is to make sure you that are aware of your location as you approach. To do this drill, start 5 to 10 yards from the wall. Push off of the bottom and begin kicking toward the wall to get a feel for the rhythm of your approach. Touch the wall with both hands about shoulder-width apart.

Now, try the drill again, but this time add one or two armstrokes. Adjust your distance until you have a good feel for your momentum and your location relative to the wall. Elite swimmers do this drill countless times to avoid being short or long on the turn.

TO INCREASE DIFFICULTY

- Start farther out, at measured distances.

TO DECREASE DIFFICULTY

- Start one stroke away.

Success Check

- You are in a streamlined position and transition flat to the surface.
- You can go at least to the flags—that is, 5 yards—with either a pull out or dolphin kick before surfacing.
- You can do the drill with both flutter and dolphin kicks.

Score Your Success

1 point: You can go 7 yards.

3 points: You can go 10 yards.

5 points: You can go 15 yards on three strokes after the streamline and breakout.

7 points: You can go more than 20 yards on three strokes after the streamline and breakout.

Two-Hand Touch-Turn Drill 2   Tall-Small-Tall Exchange

This drill helps you understand how your momentum is exchanged in the two-hand touch turn. It is performed by swimming either the breaststroke or the butterfly from 10 yards out. Gear your approach to be long and tall coming into the wall while paying close attention to the markings on the bottom of the pool. Once your hands touch, bend your elbows to allow your momentum to carry you into the wall while driving your knees to your chest; make yourself as small as possible. After your feet get to the wall, push off and make yourself tall again with a tight streamline.

TO INCREASE DIFFICULTY

- Start farther out, at measured distances.

TO DECREASE DIFFICULTY

- Start one stroke away.

Success Check

- You are in a streamlined position as you come into the wall.
- You have your hands and feet on the wall at different times.
- You can do the push-off so that it and the streamline carry you beyond 10 yards.

Score Your Success

1 point: You are fully extended going into the wall but must grab the gutter or deck to pull yourself forward.

3 points: You are fully extended going in to the wall and are able to get your feet on the wall without your hands grabbing the gutter to pull you in.

5 points: You can fully extend, rotate so that your feet and hands are not on the wall at the same time, and push off underwater.

7 points: You can go more than 10 yards after the exchange on just the push.

Two-Hand Touch-Turn Drill 3
Hand-Touch Side-to-Front Streamline

This drill is performed in four stages. Before you begin, position yourself with your head, knees, and toes up. Get one arm down in the water and pointing toward the end the pool and the other arm on the gutter. Next, release your gutter hand, stab it over your head to meet your other hand, and sink.

The second stage involves pushing off of the wall in a streamlined position with your head down to control depth. The key here is to push off forcefully and go as far as you can. Find markers in the pool or use another means to determine where you come up each time. This is only a push and a streamline—no kicking or other movements.

In the third stage, glide as far as you can. In the fourth, rotate from the side to the front while gliding and using only body control, then initiate the kick. Since you are on your side for the turn, practice rotating from the side to the front several times.

TO INCREASE DIFFICULTY

- Combine this drill with the approach and exchange drills.

TO DECREASE DIFFICULTY

- Just sink to the streamlined position in any way you prefer and push.

Success Check

- You are in a streamlined position before you push.
- You can go at least to the flags—that is, 5 yards—with no movement before surfacing.
- You can initiate one kick and be prepared to break out by being close to the surface.

Score Your Success

1 point: You can go 5 yards.

3 points: You can go 7 yards.

5 points: You can go 10 yards.

7 points: You can go 12 yards.

Two-Hand Touch-Turn Drill 4 *Two-Stroke Sprint Breakout*

After you have mastered the preceding drills, it is time to finish the turn by making a transition from streamlining to swimming. The purpose of this drill is to maintain the momentum you generated by pushing off of the wall. Many swimmers lose momentum during the breakout, and it is important to maintain as much velocity as you can.

This drill is performed by pushing off and either getting into a kicking rhythm for the butterfly or initiating a kick for the breaststroke. Next, push your chin forward to rise to the surface, then take two quick strokes. Practice this drill with varying streamline lengths to see what is most comfortable and efficient and stop after two strokes. Do the drill with both the butterfly and the breaststroke.

TO INCREASE DIFFICULTY

• Add more strokes.

TO DECREASE DIFFICULTY

• Start with only one stroke.

Success Check

• You are in a streamlined position before you push.
• You can go at least to the flags—that is, 5 yards—with specific kicks before surfacing.
• You can do the drill with both the butterfly and the breaststroke.
• You can go halfway down the pool—that is, 12.5 yards—with two strokes.

Score Your Success

1 point: You can go 5 yards.

3 points: You can go 7 yards.

5 points: You can go 10 yards.

7 points: You can go 12 yards.

FLIP TURN

The flip turn (figure 7.9) is used most commonly in freestyle and backstroke competition but is also widely used by recreational and fitness swimmers. Though competitors initially used the open turn, the flip turn has proven to be faster and more efficient.

As with the other two turns, the flip turn involves four key elements. The approach in the flip turn differs from the approach in the other two turns. The exchange involves changing the position of your head and feet; in fact, you are faceup to the surface of the water, a position in which many people experience water flowing into the nose. This annoyance can be prevented by using a nose clip or by exhaling slowly through the nose throughout the turn.

The streamline and breakout in the flip turn are the same as in the open turn. The backstroke is a little more complicated, but the movement is the same. After you swim under the backstroke flags and take three strokes, roll over onto your front and perform the same freestyle turn. The streamline is on the back with no roll to the front.

Figure 7.9 FLIP TURN

Preparation

1. Start several yards from the wall and swim a few strokes freestyle.
2. Pay close attention to the turn-target markings (if the pool has them) on the bottom and side of the pool at the end of the lane.
3. When approaching the turn target or T on the bottom markings, take your last stroke. If there is no turn target, lift your head to spot the wall and gauge the distance.
4. As you take your last stroke into the wall, both hands are at or near your hips in freestyle.
5. Tuck your chin to your chest and reach for your toes.

Execution

1. Your hands stay almost stationary in the water as your body bends at the waist. Your legs are then thrown over, at which point you find the wall with your feet.
2. Your hands are naturally above your head at this point.
3. Push off on your back, rotate to your front, and break out as you would for an open turn.

MISSTEP

You use your arms in a circular motion to help with rotation.

CORRECTION

As you take the last pull, leave both hands at your sides and slide them down to your feet while tucking your chin.

MISSTEP

You end up with your head pointed toward the bottom of the pool.

CORRECTION

Keep your chin tucked to your chest until your feet are on the wall.

DRILLS FOR FLIP TURN

Many swimmers misconceive the flip turn as simply a somersault that is easy to perform. There is, of course, more to it. A successful flip turn depends on keeping your hands stationary and using your core for the turn. The following drills help you keep your core engaged and avoid relying on your hands and arms to manipulate the water.

Flip-Turn Drill 1   Kickboard

The purpose of this drill is to keep your hands in the same place while doing the flip turn. To perform the drill, hold the bottom of a kickboard in each hand. Starting in the middle of the pool, lie on the water facedown with your hands and the kickboards at your sides and your palms and thumbs up. Tuck your chin to your chest and give a little dolphin kick while you bend at the waist. Throw your feet over so that you end up faceup at the top of the water with your arms above your head.

TO INCREASE DIFFICULTY

- Perform the drill without kickboards.

TO DECREASE DIFFICULTY

- Have a partner help your feet over.

Success Check

- You can do the drill with your hands staying in the same place.
- You can do the drill multiple times.
- You can do the drill without kickboards.

Score Your Success

1 point: You can do the drill once.

3 points: You can do the drill multiple times.

5 points: You can do the drill once without kickboards.

7 points: You can do the drill multiple times without kickboards.

Flip-Turn Drill 2   Lane Line

This drill accustoms you to bending at the waist and using your hips as the pivot point for the exchange. To do the drill, lie facedown across a lane line with your arms extended over your head; position yourself so that the lane line crosses your chest at armpit level. Next, pull both hands down to your thighs and tuck your chin to your chest while reaching for your toes over the lane line. This action pulls you forward over the lane line; when your hips reach the line, initiate the flip. Throw your feet over while bending your legs slightly. Finish in the same position, lying on your back, as in the previous drill.

TO INCREASE DIFFICULTY

- Perform the drill without a lane line.

TO DECREASE DIFFICULTY

- Have a partner help your feet over.

Success Check

- You can do the drill with your hands staying in the same place.
- You can do the drill multiple times.
- You can do the drill without a lane line.

Score Your Success

1 point: You can do the drill once.

3 points: You can do the drill multiple times.

5 points: You can do the drill once without a lane line.

7 points: You can do the drill multiple times without a lane line.

Flip-Turn Drill 3   Flags In

This drill helps you determine your ideal turn distance from the wall. Turn too soon and you miss the wall with your feet altogether. Turn too late and you're left scrunched up and unable to get a good push—or, worse, you hit your heels on the deck or gutter. To perform the drill, start in shallow water right at the backstroke flags. Push forward and take one stroke before initiating the turn. Pay careful attention to the markings on the pool bottom. Repeat this drill by adding a stroke each time until you find the right spot, then repeat the drill with your ideal number of strokes. Once you flip, find the wall with your feet, holding your knees slightly bent, and push off in a streamlined position.

TO INCREASE DIFFICULTY

• Start from the center of the pool.

• Practice at a variety of swimming speeds.

TO DECREASE DIFFICULTY

• Have a partner help your feet over.

• Have a partner tap you on your head at the right distance from the wall.

Success Check

• You can do the drill with your hands staying in the same place.

• You can do the drill multiple times.

• You can do the drill and push off in a streamline.

• You can do the drill from the middle of the pool.

Score Your Success

1 point: You can do the drill once.

3 points: You can do the drill multiple times.

5 points: You can do the drill once from the middle of the pool.

7 points: You can do the drill multiple times from the middle of the pool.

SUCCESS SUMMARY

Turns are crucial in pool swimming, and you have learned three types of turn. Now calculate your score and see just how effective you are at exchanging your momentum and changing direction.

SCORE YOUR SUCCESS

If you scored at least 40 points, then you have completed this step. If you scored 41 to 55 points, then you are well on your way and have the potential to develop your swimming stroke even further. If you scored more than 55 points, then you have mastered the key elements for taking your swimming to the next level.

Open Turn Drills

1.	Approach	___ out of 5
2.	Exchange	___ out of 5
3.	Side-to-Front Streamline	___ out of 7
4.	1-2-3 Streamlines	___ out of 7
5.	Three-Stroke Spin	___ out of 7

Two-Hand Touch Turn Drills

1.	Approach	___ out of 7
2.	Tall-Small-Tall Exchange	___ out of 7
3.	Hand-Touch Side-to-Front Streamline	___ out of 7
4.	Two-Stroke Sprint Breakout	___ out of 7

Flip-Turn Drills

1.	Kickboard	___ out of 7
2.	Lane Line	___ out of 7
3.	Flags In	___ out of 7
	Total	___ **out of 80**

Starts

Starts are used primarily in competitive swimming, but recreational swimmers and fitness swimmers can also benefit from knowing how to perform a good start. In competitive swimming, starting involves performing a sequence of movements to generate as much velocity as possible down the length of the pool. After all, this is the last chance to push against something solid (until the turn) and to benefit from gravity, so it pays to make the most of it.

For all of the strokes covered in this book, the start consists of four basic elements: 1) set, 2) push, 3) entry, and 4) streamline.

The set is the posture that you take on the side of the pool or on the starting block. The push is the explosive movement that generates velocity down the pool. The entry is the transition into the water, and the streamline is how you carry that momentum into the water in order to use it as swimming speed.

IN-WATER STARTS

Of course, many swimmers do not compete, but start skills are still important for them. Beginners and others who cannot dive should look at the sections addressing the streamline and the breakout in the stroke-specific discussions. In-water starts involve simply pushing off from the wall, and they are perfectly legal in most competitions. The rules do specify that you must have at least one hand on the wall and must push off of the wall rather than contacting the bottom of the pool.

DIVE STARTS

Before you begin this step, make certain that the pool you are using is a safe place to perform a dive start. Many pools either restrict diving or are not deep enough for diving at all. Check with the lifeguard or your instructor to ensure that this particular activity is appropriate at your pool. Depth requirements vary from governing body to governing body, but all require at least 4.5 feet (~1.4 m); if you are a novice, then even deeper is better. And again, before attempting *any* dive start, check with the facility or safety staff—the risk of head or neck injury during a dive start is much greater in shallow water.

Although many people know how to dive, the competitive dive start is a little different from just diving in to get wet on a hot day. Even if you are an experienced swimmer, it is good to have a refresher in the elements of diving.

A dive start is an attempt to maximize velocity and minimize drag at the start of a contest. Since all of our strokes are headfirst, diving in headfirst (or rather hands first) prevents any waste of energy from changing position. Ideally, a dive start involves very little vertical content, thus directing the explosive movement down the length of the pool. The transition into the water consists of angling down toward the water, leading with the hands, and following with the rest of the body at an ideal angle for achieving the best depth—not too much and not too little. The following progression gets you used to the proper entry position.

KNEELING DIVE

The first part of the progression is the kneeling dive (figure 8.1). During this part, many swimmers place a towel on the deck to protect their knees. Repeat the process several times before moving on; each time, try to enter through the "hole" that your hands make in the water.

Figure 8.1   KNEELING DIVE

Set

1. Kneel at the edge of the pool deck facing the water on one knee and your other leg up and the toes of that foot wrapped around the edge of the deck or coping.
2. Place your hands over your head in a streamlined position and squeeze your ears with your biceps.
3. Bend at your waist toward the water while keeping your head down.

Push

1. As you roll into the water hands first, keep your chin tucked and push out (not up) with your non-kneeling leg.

Entry

1. As you enter the water, maintain your streamlined position.

Streamline

1. Streamline as you would with any forward stroke.

STANDING DIVE

The standing dive (figure 8.2) is similar to the kneeling dive, but of course this time your head and hands are farther from the water. Repeat the entire process several times before moving on; each time, try to enter through the hole that your hands make in the water.

Figure 8.2 STANDING DIVE

Set

1. Stand at the edge of the pool and assume the streamlined vertical position.
2. Bend at your waist with your head down as you point your hands toward the water.

Push

1. As you roll into the water hands first, keep your chin tucked and push with both feet.

Entry

1. As you enter the water, maintain your streamlined position.

Streamline

1. Streamline as you would with any forward stroke.

MISSTEP

You look up and belly flop.

CORRECTION

Keep your chin tucked to your chest the whole time.

MISSTEP

You push off too soon and your feet go in first.

CORRECTION

Remember that your feet are the last thing to move, doing so after you are almost into the water with your hands.

MISSTEP

You end up being too deep or too shallow on your entry.

CORRECTION

Adjust how far out you point your hands as you roll into the water.

DIVE-START EQUIPMENT

Before transitioning from the deck to the starting block, there are few things to consider. First, not every facility has starting blocks, and those that do often place restrictions on who is allowed to use them and under what circumstances. If you are permitted to use the block—and if you have successful experience in diving from the side of the pool—then you may want to begin working from the block. Starting blocks traditionally stand 20 to 30 inches (0.5-0.75 m) above the water. This may not seem like a great height, but it adds a lot of energy to the start and makes pool depth all the more important. Though traditionally performed from a starting block, this forward dive start can also be done from the side of the pool.

Starting blocks may be either removable or permanently installed. They come in a variety of designs, depending on the manufacturer, but generally include a platform angled slightly forward or down toward the water. Some also include a wedge at the back, and this feature is currently considered state of the art for competitive racing blocks. Let's turn now to the various dive starts.

FORWARD OR GRAB START

The forward or grab start (figure 8.3) can be done from the deck or from a block and is used for freestyle, breaststroke, and butterfly. To perform it, stand at the front edge of the block with your toes curled over the edge, then bend at your waist and bend your knees slightly. Next, grab the front edge of the block with both hands; it is very important to keep your neck loose and look down or only slightly forward.

This is the set position, in which you should be reasonably comfortable with your center of gravity directly above your feet and ankles. As your feet leave the block, your hips, knees, and ankles should all be on the same line, parallel to the surface of the water, in order to generate maximum forward velocity. Your upper body is angled toward your entry position and your fingers are pointed directly to that spot.

As your feet enter the water, you should be 2 to 2.5 feet (0.6-0.75 m) under the surface. It will take several attempts to find your ideal depth, which depends on which stroke you are swimming and what is most comfortable to you. After your feet enter the water, you are in the streamline phase. Perform this part of the start as described in the stroke-specific step chapters.

Remember that at the instant you enter the water, you are traveling at the fastest speed you will achieve in your swim. Therefore, it is crucial to achieve a tight streamline in order to avoid slowing down and to minimize drag. The streamline for freestyle and butterfly involves powerful kicking at very high frequency, whereas the breaststroke streamline involves the breaststroke pullout.

The breakout, once again, is the transition from streamlining to swimming. In all of these strokes, the first few strokes after the streamline are crucial for maintaining the momentum you generated in the start and the streamline. To do so, focus on making your first few strokes powerful and flawless.

Figure 8.3 FORWARD OR GRAB START

Set

1. Stand at the front edge of the block with your toes curled over the edge.
2. Bend at your waist and bend your knees slightly.
3. Grab the front edge of the block with both hands.
4. Very important: Keep your neck loose and look down or only slightly forward.

Push

1. At the start command, initiate the start by pulling forward with your hands while simultaneously driving forward with your upper body.
2. Lift your head slightly to spot the water and the point at which you hope to enter.

3. At the same time, bring your hands forward toward the streamlined position.
4. Now tuck your chin to your chest in the streamlined position.

Entry

1. As your hands enter the water, begin to straighten your body so that it goes into the same hole in the water that your hands entered.
2. As your body passes through the surface of the water, arch your back slightly to control the depth of the dive.

Streamline

1. Push your chin forward slightly to adjust your depth and bring you to the surface for swimming as you streamline and kick as appropriate for the chosen stroke.

MISSTEP

Your hands are separated when you enter.

CORRECTION

Make sure to bring your hands forward to the streamlined position immediately after the start command.

MISSTEP

You spear up on the breakout and almost come to a stop.

CORRECTION

Make sure that you come to the surface for the breakout almost parallel to the surface.

MISSTEP

You "pancake" or hit the water flat.

CORRECTION

Spot your entry a little closer to the block.

MISSTEP

You "submarine" or go too deep on the entry.

CORRECTION

Spot your entry a little farther from the block.

DRILLS FOR FORWARD OR GRAB START

Performing a good forward start depends on your ability to generate a great deal of horizontal force and maintain the velocity generated by pushing off of something solid from a significant height. The following drills help you master the forward start by emphasizing each component of a good start.

Forward or Grab Start Drill 1   Standing Jump

This feetfirst drill isolates the push to help you generate explosive power from either the pool deck or a starting block. From the take-your-mark position, instead of pulling forward with your hands, let go and swing your arms forward. At the same time, push forward as forcefully as possible to get as much forward velocity as you can, then pull your feet up to enter the water feetfirst. Practice this drill several times to see how far down the pool you can get.

In competition, start sequencing may vary in several ways. Most meets use whistle commands. First, a series of short whistles from the starter or another official calls competitors to the block. A long whistle then signals them to step up on the block (or into the water in the case of backstroke) and get ready to assume the start position. The starter then tells competitors to take their marks, at which time they need to get into the start position and hold it. The start of the race itself is signaled by a horn or whistle.

TO INCREASE DIFFICULTY

- Place a marker (e.g., a diving brick) on the bottom of the pool as a target and aim for the spot in the water directly above it.

TO DECREASE DIFFICULTY

- Start from the deck and just do the drill as a standing broad jump.
- Start from the deck in the set position.

Success Check

- You can hold yourself steady in the set position.
- You can enter the water at least four feet (1.2 m) away from the block.
- You can hit a target in the water after spotting it.

Score Your Success

1 point: You can do the drill from the deck and enter at least one yard from the wall.

3 points: You can do the drill and enter at least 4 feet (1.2 m) from the wall.

5 points: You can do the drill and enter at a target spot at least 4 feet (1.2 m) from the wall.

Forward or Grab Start Drill 2 Streamline Only

Once you have mastered this drill, it is time to work on the entry. This drill isolates the entry portion of the start. It is performed by standing on the block, assuming the take-your-mark position, performing the push, and then going as far as you can with no movement—just a streamline. This drill not only maximizes your push force but also ensures that you make a good entry and carry as much momentum as possible into the water. Experiment with different depths and entry positions until you find what works best for you.

TO INCREASE DIFFICULTY

- Hold the streamlined position until you come to a stop.

TO DECREASE DIFFICULTY

- Kick while streamlining.

Success Check

- You can perform the drill without pancaking or submarining.
- Your feet, hips, and shoulders are all at the same level in the water after you enter.
- You achieve a streamlined position and go at least 10 yards.

Score Your Success

1 point: You can do the drill and go 5 yards.

3 points: You can do the drill and go 10 yards.

5 points: You can do the drill and go at least half the length of the pool with no kicking or other body movement.

Once you have mastered this drill, it is time to work on the breakout, which is critical in maintaining the momentum you generate off of the block and during the entry. In a race, a bad breakout can bring you almost to a complete stop, whereas a good one can put you ahead. The following drill helps you work on making a smooth transition from streamline to swimming.

Breakout Drill 1   Kick to the Break

This drill helps you build on your mastery of the preceding drills by concentrating on the transition from the streamline to swimming. As you have learned, a great deal of momentum is lost with any nonstreamlined position or movement. To perform this drill, do the set, push, and entry and then add vigorous and high-frequency kicking. As you make your way down the pool underwater, push your chin forward and feel yourself rise. When you break the surface, stop. If you are doing the breaststroke, perform one pullout and rise to the surface. Take note of your position in the pool each time you finish the drill.

TO INCREASE DIFFICULTY

- Take your first stroke.

TO DECREASE DIFFICULTY

- Don't kick.

Success Check

- You can be in a streamlined position before you push.
- You can go at least to the flags—that is, five yards—before surfacing.
- Your head, shoulders, and hips all break the surface at the same time.

Score Your Success

1 point: You can go 5 yards.

3 points: You can go 7 yards.

5 points: You can go 10 yards.

7 points: You can go 12 yards.

TRACK START

The track start (figure 8.4) was developed in the 1950s by a few athletes who tinkered around with it during practices and local competitions. The difference in the track start is the start position. In this position, one foot is forward and the other is back, just like track athletes use for their starts. During the 1960s and 1970s, it was used by some U.S. collegiate swimmers, and in the 1980s a few U.S. swimmers became the first to use it in international competition. They were disqualified, but a challenge to the ruling led to the conclusion that regulations did not require both feet to be at the front of the starting blocks. By the 1990s, the technique had become more widespread, and it is now the standard starting technique for most swimmers. It can be done from the deck or from a block, and it is used in freestyle, breaststroke, and butterfly.

Figure 8.4 TRACK START

Set

1. Stand at the front edge of the block with one foot forward and the toes curled over the edge.
2. Place your other foot at the back of the block.
3. Bend at your waist and bend your knees slightly to assume almost a crouched position.
4. Grab the front edge of the block with both hands.
5. Very important: Keep your neck loose and look down or only slightly forward. Keep your center of gravity comfortably over the center of the block, between your forward foot and your back foot.

Push

1. At the start command, initiate the start by pulling forward with your hands while simultaneously driving forward with your upper body.

2. Lift your head slightly to spot the water and the point at which you hope to enter.
3. At the same time, bring your hands forward toward the streamlined position.
4. Then tuck your chin to your chest in the streamlined position.

Entry

1. As your hands enter the water, begin to straighten your body so that it goes into the same hole in the water that your hands entered.
2. As your body passes through the surface of the water, arch your back slightly to control the depth of the dive.

Streamline

1. Push your chin forward slightly to adjust the depth and bring you to the surface for swimming as you streamline and perform the appropriate kick for the chosen stroke.

Which foot is the best foot to put forward? To answer this question, use the following simple methods. First, have a partner or your coach stand behind you. Stand with your own feet together, close your eyes, and have the other person gently push you forward. Whichever leg moves first to stop you from falling is your dominant leg. This fact alone, however, does not make it the best foot to put forward.

Next, have the other person observe whether your hips are back or forward in your set position. People whose hips sit a little back tend to be faster on the start when they put the dominant leg forward; those whose hips sit forward tend to do better with the nondominant leg forward. In either case, your feet should point straight down the pool rather than at any kind of angle. Ultimately, of course, the only way to tell for sure which approach is right for you is to try them out and see which one gets you farther down the pool.

After your feet enter the water, you are in the streamline phase. Perform this part of the start as described for each stroke in previous steps. Remember that the instant you enter the water, you are traveling at the fastest speed you will achieve in your swim. Therefore, it is crucial to achieve a tight streamline in order to avoid slowing down and to minimize drag. The streamline for freestyle and butterfly involves powerful kicking at very high frequency, whereas the breaststroke streamline involves the breaststroke pullout.

The breakout, once again, is the transition phase from streamlining to swimming. As mentioned earlier, push your chin forward slightly to adjust your depth and bring you to the surface for swimming.

In all of these swimming strokes, your first few strokes after the streamline are crucial for maintaining the momentum you generated in the start and the streamline. To do so, focus on making your first few strokes powerful and flawless. In addition, this particular type of start involves a few more variables that must be managed. Whether you have your hips forward or back, your timing, and the amount of vertical force you put into the start all influence the entry. If your feet do not enter through the same hole in the water as the rest of the body, you may twist, which will influence the way you streamline. You may have to make adjustments with your body and in your streamline to ensure that you can manage the breakout effectively.

MISSTEP

You look up, lose your balance, and fall in.

CORRECTION

Keep your neck loose; looking at the end of the pool constricts blood vessels in the neck.

MISSTEP

You rock back too far and sit on your back leg.

CORRECTION

Having the hips slightly forward or back is common and often merely a matter of preference. However, a knee bend of more than 90 degrees does not allow for a good push. Move your hips forward.

MISSTEP

Your front leg is straight and locked out.

CORRECTION

Make sure that you bend your knee so that you have some way of pushing off of the block with your lead leg rather than just your foot.

DRILLS FOR THE TRACK START

The next few drills focus on connecting all of the skills of the set, push, entry, and breakout streamline into one integrated skill.

Track Start Drill 1   15-Meter

Though not really a drill, this exercise enables you to determine which start is best for you. Try the grab start and record your time at 15 yards. Do the same for the track start with each leg serving as the forward leg. Do this sequence several times to determine which type of start is best for you.

In competition pools, the 15-yard mark is signified by an off-color (e.g., red or yellow) disk as part of the lane line. If the pool does not have such a mark, you can use any measured distance beyond 10 yards.

Track Start Drill 2   Standing Jump

This drill isolates the push portion of the start. From the take-your-mark position, push forward as forcefully as possible to get as much forward velocity as you can. Then pull your feet up to enter the water feetfirst. Practice this drill several times to see how far down the pool you can get.

TO INCREASE DIFFICULTY

- Place a marker (e.g., a diving brick) on the bottom of the pool as a target and try to hit the spot in the water directly above it.

TO DECREASE DIFFICULTY

- Start from the deck and just do the drill as a standing broad jump.
- Start from the deck in the set position.

Success Check

- You can hold yourself steady in the set position.
- You can enter the water at least 4 feet (1.2 m) away from the block.
- You can hit a target in the water after spotting it.

Score Your Success

1 point: You can do the drill from the deck and get at least a yard from the wall.

3 points: You can do the drill and get at least 4 feet (1.2 m) from the wall.

5 points: You can do the drill and hit a designated target at least 4 feet (1.2 m) from the wall.

ENTRY DRILLS

Once you have mastered the standing jump drill, it is time to work on the entry. Your entry is crucial for maintaining the power that you generate off of the block. If you go too shallow, you belly flop; if your angle is too severe, you go to the bottom of the pool. On the other hand, the proper angle of entry—along with a good streamline— gets you down the pool with the most efficiency and speed.

Entry Drill Streamline Only

This drill isolates the entry portion of the start. It is performed by standing on the block, getting into the take-your-mark position, performing the push, and going as far as you can with no movement—just a streamline. The drill not only maximizes your push force but also ensures that you make a good entry and carry as much momentum as possible into the water. Experiment with different depths and entry positions to find what works best for you.

TO INCREASE DIFFICULTY

• Hold the streamlined position until you come to a stop.

TO DECREASE DIFFICULTY

• Kick while streamlining.

Success Check

• You can perform the drill without pancaking or submarining.
• Your feet, hips, and shoulders are all at the same level in the water after you enter.
• You are in a streamlined position and can go at least 10 yards.

Score Your Success

1 point: You can do the drill and go 5 yards.

3 points: You can do the drill and go 10 yards.

5 points: You can do the drill and go at least half of the pool length with no kicking or other movement.

Once you have mastered this drill, it is time to work on the breakout.

Breakout Drill   Kick to the Break

This drill helps you build on your mastery of the preceding drills by concentrating on the transition from the streamline to swimming. As you have learned, a great deal of momentum is lost with any nonstreamlined position or movement. To perform this drill, do the set, push, and entry and then add vigorous and high-frequency kicking. As you make your way down the pool underwater, push your chin forward and feel yourself rise. When you break the surface, stop. If you are doing the breaststroke, perform one pullout and rise to the surface. Take note of your position in the pool each time you finish the drill.

TO INCREASE DIFFICULTY

- Take your first stroke.

TO DECREASE DIFFICULTY

- Don't kick.

Success Check

- You can be in a streamlined position before you push.
- You can go at least to the flags—that is, 5 yards—before surfacing.
- Your head, shoulders, and hips all break the surface at the same time.

Score Your Success

1 point: You can go 5 yards.

3 points: You can go 7 yards.

5 points: You can go 10 yards.

7 points: You can go 12 yards.

BACKSTROKE CURL START

Backstroke differs considerably from the chest-down swimming strokes, and the start (figure 8.5) is no exception. The backstroke start can be performed from the deck or a block; either way, it is done in the water with the feet on the wall and the back facing down the pool. For the entry, push off and do a back "dive," which brings you underwater and sets up the streamline.

An effective backstroke start begins, of course, with the set. Competitive blocks are outfitted with grab bars for backstroke, but even then some swimmers opt to use the deck. The set is performed by placing the feet flat on the wall with the elbows bent.

Next comes the push, for which the key is timing. The result should be almost a back dive. The most efficient swimmers follow an arc and their feet go from under the water to out of the water and then back through the same hole that the upper body goes through. Strong swimmers get the entire body out of the water at some point and basically go through the same hole as the hands.

Depth on the entry differs from that of the chest-down strokes. In the backstroke, the streamline and the dolphin kick are important elements. In fact, one of the fastest recorded backstroke swims was done mostly on an underwater streamline with a dolphin kick. With this in mind, if you are a good dolphin kicker, it works to your advantage to go deeper and longer on the entry. In competition, your streamline is allowed to extend for a maximum of 15 yards. Experiment to find out which head and body positions produce the best streamline for you while keeping you underwater for the correct amount of streamline.

Since you are faceup, it is likely that water will go up your nose unless you breathe out slowly. Alternatively, some swimmers opt for a nose clip.

Figure 8.5 BACKSTROKE CURL START

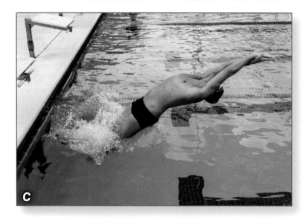

Set

1. Enter the water feetfirst and face the wall.
2. Place your feet on the wall about shoulder-width apart so that your back faces down the pool.
3. Rather than using just your forefeet or toes, position your feet closer to the surface of the water and flatter on the wall.
4. Your hands should be on the grab bar or deck. In the set position, keep your hips away from the wall and curl your back and shoulders toward the block.

Push

1. Your upper body and shoulders must be moving down the pool before your feet push. As a result, you must push away from the grab bars and throw your hands either over your head or out to the side to bring them to the streamlined position.
2. The motion should involve pointing your fingers down toward the bottom of the pool over your head.
3. Your head follows your shoulders, and your back should arch as you then push with your legs.

Entry

1. Make the entry fingers-first with your head back.
2. Strong swimmers get the entire body out of the water at some point and basically go through the same hole as the hands.

Streamline

1. In backstroke, the streamline is done on the back; do not roll over during this phase.
2. Breathe out slowly to prevent water from entering your nose.
3. The dolphin kick is often the preferred method of kicking underwater, but a flutter kick is more effective for some swimmers.

MISSTEP

You throw your head back and go too deep.

CORRECTION

Remember to keep your neck loose and envision your shoulders going first.

MISSTEP

You push off at the same time that you let go of the grab bars and therefore pancake the start.

CORRECTION

Remember to push away and arch your back before you push.

MISSTEP

You sit on your heels and then your feet slip down the wall on the start.

CORRECTION

Make sure that your hips face down the pool and that your knees are bent at about 90 degrees. Be sure that your shoulders are past your hips before pushing.

DRILLS FOR BACKSTROKE CURL START

The following drills isolate each part of the start in order to help you perform the skill effectively. One caveat: Many people find it uncomfortable to be upside down and unable to see where they are going. Please make sure that the lane is clear before you try these drills. Rest assured that the more you do them, the more comfortable you get.

Backstroke Curl Drill 1   Back Flip

One of the most difficult parts of the start is to avoid a flat or pancake start. Foot positioning will allow you to produce maximum force horizontally down the pool. Some years ago, many swimmers—the rules allowed this—curled their toes over the gutter to get a little extra vertical force to almost do a back dive into the water. While you are not allowed to curl your toes over the gutter or deck, it is a good idea to place your feet as close as you can to the top of the water.

This drill is performed by throwing your hands and arms back, almost as if trying to touch the bottom of the pool behind you. This action requires you to arch your back more than you do on a regular start. You must also attend to your head positioning; specifically, make sure to look back toward the bottom of the pool behind you. If you end up vertical with your head down, then you have done the drill correctly.

(continued)

Backstroke Curl Drill 1 *(continued)*

TO INCREASE DIFFICULTY

• Try to get all the way over.

TO DECREASE DIFFICULTY

• Have a partner hold your feet to the wall and then throw them up.

Success Check

• You can do the drill with your feet exiting the water and then reentering.

• You can do the drill multiple times and reach toward the bottom of the pool upside down.

• You can do the drill, make a complete circle, and come back to the start position facing the wall.

Score Your Success

1 point: You can do the drill but are still faceup upon entry.

3 points: You can do the drill and are vertical with your head down.

5 points: You can do the drill multiple times and are vertical with your head down.

7 points: You can do the drill multiple times, making a complete inverted circle and coming back to face the wall.

Backstroke Curl Drill 2 Backstroke Streamline

This drill isolates the entry portion of the start. To perform it, do the set and then the push; after entry, go as far as you can with no body movements—just a streamline. This drill not only maximizes your push force but also ensures that you make a good entry and carry as much momentum as possible into the water. Experiment with different depths and entry positions until you find what works best for you.

TO INCREASE DIFFICULTY

• Hold the streamlined position until you come to a stop.

TO DECREASE DIFFICULTY

• Kick while streamlining.

Success Check

• You can perform the drill without pancaking or submarining.

• Your feet, hips, and shoulders are all at the same level in the water after you enter.

• You achieve a streamlined position and go at least 10 yards.

Score Your Success

1 point: You can do the drill and go 5 yards.

3 points: You can do the drill and go 10 yards.

5 points: You can do the drill and go at least half of the pool length with no kicking or other movement.

Breakout Drill   Kick to the Break

This drill helps you build on your mastery of the preceding drills by concentrating on the transition from the streamline to swimming. As you have learned, a great deal of momentum is lost with any nonstreamlined position or movement. To perform this drill, do the set, push, and entry and then add vigorous and high-frequency kicking. Deeper is better, and longer is better if you are a good dolphin kicker. When you break the surface, stop.

TO INCREASE DIFFICULTY

- Take your first stroke.
- Go at least 15 yards.

TO DECREASE DIFFICULTY

- Flutter-kick.

Success Check

- You can be in a streamlined position before you push.
- You can go at least to the flags—that is, 5 yards—before surfacing.
- Your head, shoulders, and hips all break the surface at the same time.

Score Your Success

1 point: You can go 5 yards.

3 points: You can go 7 yards.

5 points: You can go 10 yards.

7 points: You can go 12 yards.

FLAT-BACK START

The flat-back start (figure 8.6) is similar in many respects to the curl start. It differs mainly in the set, wherein the hips are closer to the wall and the shoulders are farther down the pool.

Next comes the push, for which the key is timing. The motion should involve pointing your fingers down toward the bottom of the pool over your head. The result should be almost a back dive. The most efficient swimmers follow an arc and their feet go from under the water to out of the water and then back through the same hole that the upper body goes through. Strong swimmers get the entire body out of the water at some point and basically go through the same hole as the hands.

Depth on the entry differs from that of the chest-down strokes. In the backstroke, the streamline and dolphin kick are important elements. In fact, one of the fastest recorded backstroke swims was done mostly on an underwater streamline with a dolphin kick. With this in mind, if you are a good dolphin kicker, it works to your advantage to go deeper and longer on the entry. Experiment to find out which head and body positions produce the best streamline for you while keeping you underwater for the correct amount of streamline. To prevent water from entering your nose during this phase, breathe out slowly or use a nose clip.

Figure 8.6 **FLAT-BACK START**

Set

1. Your set should be the same as the curl start with your feet about shoulder-width apart.
2. In the set position, keep your hips away from the wall and your back flat and farther away from the block than your hips are.

Push

1. Your upper body and shoulders must be moving down the pool before your feet push. As a result, you must push away from the grab bars and throw your hands either over your head or out to the side to bring them to the streamlined position.
2. Your head follows your shoulders, and your back should arch as you then push with your legs.

Entry

1. Make the entry fingers-first with your head back.
2. Strong swimmers kick the feet in the air off of the wall and go through the same hole in the water that the hands go through.

Streamline

1. As before, you are allowed only 15 yards of underwater streamline.
2. To prevent water from entering your nose, breathe out slowly or use a nose clip.

MISSTEP

You push your hips forward first.

CORRECTION

Remember to push after you initiate the shoulder movement down the pool.

MISSTEP

You sit on your heels and cannot accelerate the push.

CORRECTION

Make sure that your knees are bent and that your hips are still closer to the wall than your shoulders are.

DRILLS FOR FLAT-BACK START

One of the most difficult parts of the start is to avoid a flat or pancake start. Foot positioning will allow you to produce maximum force horizontally down the pool. Some years ago, many swimmers—the rules allowed this—curled their toes over the gutter to get a little extra vertical force to almost do a back dive into the water. While you are not allowed to curl your toes over the gutter or deck, it is a good idea to place your feet as close to the top of the water as you can.

Flat-Back Start Drill 1   Back Flip

This drill is performed by throwing your hands and arms back, almost as if trying to touch the bottom of the pool behind you. This action requires you to arch your back more than you do on a regular start. You must also attend to your head positioning; specifically, make sure to look back toward the bottom of the pool behind you. If you end up vertical with your head down, then you have done the drill correctly.

TO INCREASE DIFFICULTY

- Try to get all the way over by completely flipping.

TO DECREASE DIFFICULTY

- Have a partner hold your feet to the wall and then throw them up.

Success Check

- You can do the drill with your feet exiting the water and then reentering.
- You can do the drill multiple times and reach toward the bottom of the pool upside down.
- You can do the drill, make a complete circle, and come back to the start position facing the wall.

Score Your Success

1 point: You can do the drill but are still faceup upon entry.

3 points: You can do the drill and are vertical with your head down.

5 points: You can do the drill multiple times and are vertical with your head down.

7 points: You can do the drill multiple times, making a complete inverted circle and coming back to face the wall.

Flat-Back Start Drill 2   Backstroke Streamline

This drill isolates the entry portion of the start. To perform it, do the set and then the push; after entry, go as far as you can with no movement—just a streamline. This drill not only maximizes your push force but also ensures that you make a good entry and carry as much momentum as possible into the water. Experiment with different depths and entry positions until you find what works best for you.

TO INCREASE DIFFICULTY

- Hold the streamlined position until you come to a stop.

TO DECREASE DIFFICULTY

- Kick while streamlining.

Success Check

- You can perform the drill without pancaking or submarining.
- Your feet, hips, and shoulders are all at the same level in the water after you enter.
- You are in a streamlined position and can go at least 10 yards.

Score Your Success

1 point: You can do the drill and go 5 yards.

3 points: You can do the drill and go 10 yards.

5 points: You can do the drill and go at least half of the pool length with no kicking or other movement.

Breakout Drill   Kick to the Break

This drill helps you build on your mastery of the preceding drills by concentrating on the transition from the streamline to swimming. As you have learned, a great deal of momentum is lost with any nonstreamlined position or movement. To perform this drill, do the set, push, and entry and then add vigorous and high-frequency kicking. Deeper is better, and longer is better if you are a good dolphin kicker. When you break the surface, stop.

TO INCREASE DIFFICULTY

- Take your first stroke.
- Go at least 15 yards.

TO DECREASE DIFFICULTY

- Flutter-kick.

Success Check

- You can be in a streamlined position before you push.
- You can go at least to the flags—that is, 5 yards—before surfacing.
- Your head, shoulders, and hips all break the surface at the same time.

Score Your Success

1 point: You can go 5 yards.

3 points: You can go 7 yards.

5 points: You can go 10 yards.

7 points: You can go 12 yards.

SUCCESS SUMMARY

If swim for competition, the start provides your first opportunity to gain an advantage. If you swim for recreation or fitness, the start allows you to begin with good momentum rather than struggling to get up to speed. Each drill in this step has helped you become proficient at starting.

SCORE YOUR SUCCESS

If you scored at least 25 points, then you have completed this step. If you scored 26 to 40 points, then you are well on your way and have the potential to develop your swimming stroke even further. If you scored more than 40 points, then you have mastered the key elements for taking your swimming to the next level.

Forward or Grab Start Drills

1. Standing Jump   ___ out of 5

2. Streamline Only   ___ out of 5

Breakout Drill

1. Kick to the Break   ___ out of 7

Track Start Drills

1. 15-Meter   ___ out of 5

2. Standing Jump   ___ out of 5

Entry Drill

1. Streamline Only   ___ out of 5

Breakout Drill

1. Kick to the Break   ___ out of 7

Backstroke Curl Drills

1. Back Flip   ___ out of 7

2. Backstroke Streamline Only   ___ out of 5

Breakout Drill

1. Kick to the Break   ___ out of 7

Flat-Back Start Drills

1. Back Flip   ___ out of 7

2. Backstroke Streamline   ___ out of 5

Breakout Drill

1. Kick to the Break   ___ out of 7

   Total   **___ out of 55**

Open-Water and Survival Swimming

Open-water swimming and what might be called survival swimming are the roots of today's competitive swimming. All swimming traces its history back to ancient times, when pool swimming did not exist but of course both large and small bodies of water did. Whether for sport or survival, then, this is where the bloodline of all swimming begins.

Although open-water swimming and pool swimming share similar stroke skills, they are completely different sports in many ways. For one thing, pool swimming takes place in a very controlled environment with a set distance and controlled water and air temperatures. In contrast, open-water and survival swimming take place in settings affected by variable environmental factors. This step focuses on skills and drills that are important for both competitive and recreational open-water swimming, as well as those that can help you in an emergency.

Before you start, review the following safety principles, which applies to all types of open-water swimming, whether for competition, recreation, or survival.

1. *Never* swim alone.
2. Be aware of environmental factors.
3. Plan your swim and make your plan known to others.
4. Take all appropriate safety equipment and make sure that it is in good working order.

OPEN-WATER SWIMMING: THE ENVIRONMENT

The first consideration for any open-water swim is the environment, which includes air and water temperatures, weather, surface conditions, currents, geography (of both the shore and the water beneath the surface), water quality, and any wildlife in the area. (See figure 9.1 for a basic open-water course.) Air temperature plays a role not only in the potential for hypothermia when you get out of the water but also in how quickly a body of water cools. In addition, large differences between air temperature and water temperature stress the body because the body requires energy to regulate temperature.

Of course, water temperature itself is also of great concern. Water starts feeling cold to most people around 81 degrees Fahrenheit (27 degrees Celsius) and too warm at about 85 degrees Fahrenheit (29 degrees Celsius). In international competitions, water temperatures are required to be between about 61 and 88 degrees Fahrenheit (16 and 31 degrees Celsius). Competitions with cooler temperatures often allow competitors to use wetsuits for warmth rather than requiring traditional bathing suits.

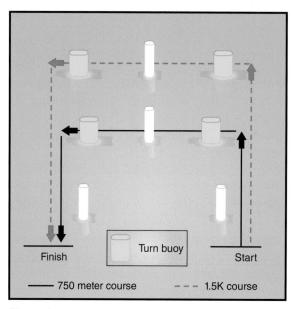

Figure 9.1 Basic open-water course.

Another environmental concern for open-water swimming is the weather. A good swim depends in part on good planning in relation to sunrise and sunset times, as well as the weather forecast for the area. Swimming in the dark is never recommended because of increased animal activity, less visibility, and colder temperatures. Open-water swimmers should also avoid inclement weather, including rain and especially thunderstorms. Fog is also a concern because it impedes navigation and can create an emergency for an otherwise accomplished swimmer.

Open-water swimmers must also consider surface conditions when planning a swim. This is especially true of larger bodies of water, in which waves and swells can be problematic; however, it is also true for smaller bodies of water, in which even a light chop of small waves can create an issue. Swells and chop are often caused by wind, but they can also be produced by other factors, such as upwellings and tidal changes.

Another—and often neglected—aspect of surface conditions involves traffic. It is not recommended that you swim in an area of high boat traffic; interactions between watercraft and swimmers usually end poorly for the swimmer. There may also be surface debris, such as sticks, logs, and trash.

An open-water swim plan must also take account of currents and of the geography—both of the bottom of the body of water and of the immediate shoreline. A swimmer can be carried offshore by a rip current or downstream by river flow, and either situation is dangerous. Therefore, it is crucial to know about any currents or tides, including their strength and direction of flow. As for geography, consider all possible factors. For example, is there a shallow entry or a drop-off? How deep is the water? Is the shore sandy or rocky? Is there any vegetation?

In addition, when swimming in a body of water other than a pool (and sometimes even in a pool!), you will encounter some form of biological life. It could be as simple as bacteria, moss, or algae or as complex and intimidating as fish, jellyfish, reptiles, or mammals. This caveat is not meant to discourage you from enjoying a swim in the open water but to stress the importance of knowing what you are getting into. Check with local officials to make sure that your intended swimming location is free from harmful bacteria and other potentially dangerous life forms. Consider also the fact that some aquatic and marine creatures follow regular patterns of daily or migratory activity. Your best sources for information about such matters are local safety experts and officials.

GETTING IN AND STARTING

Before you begin this step, make sure that your chosen body of water is a safe place for swimming. To do so, check with the lifeguard, local officials, or your instructor. In addition, it is critically important to practice all of these drills in a pool or other controlled environment before practicing in open water.

Entry

Here you bring to bear your geographical knowledge of the immediate shoreline or dock area, as well as what lies beneath the water. When entering from a dock or boat (figure 9.2), always adhere to the maxim "feet first the first time" in order to prevent injury. Once you know the starting conditions—and how you are going to enter the water—you can develop skills to help you enjoy competitive and recreational open-water swimming.

Figure 9.2 OPEN-WATER FIRST-TIME ENTRY

Preparation

1. Find a shallow-approach or zero-entry pool.
2. Wade in to a depth that reaches at least your upper thighs.

Execution

1. At the point where it is too difficult to continue wading, bring your arms to the front and push forward off of the bottom.
2. Keep your hands in front, let your feet leave the bottom, and push your chest forward. This approach allows you to cover more horizontal distance with less energy than walking.
3. Pull one knee up, find the bottom with that foot again, and repeat the upper-body motion as you draw your other leg past the first leg.
4. Repeat as often as necessary to reach a swimming depth.

The preceding skill is practiced in a zero-entry pool, but it can also be used at an open-water venue, as shown in the photos. The zero-entry pool is safer, and many skills can be practiced there first prior to open-water trials. The following missteps and corrections are for performing the drills in an open-water environment.

MISSTEP

You run into the water and promptly fall flat after tripping on a rock.

CORRECTION

Check the bottom for obstructions; ask local officials about the terrain.

MISSTEP

You start swimming and grab handfuls of bottom muck.

CORRECTION

You started swimming too early. Start with a few dolphin dives to get out to deeper water.

Compact or Stride Entry

The compact, or stride, entry (figure 9.3) is used for jumping into water of unknown depth.

Figure 9.3   COMPACT OR STRIDE ENTRY

Preparation

1. Jump in feetfirst with your knees bent and your arms extended out to your sides.
2. You will be vertical in the water and will need to get to a horizontal swimming position as quickly as possible.

Execution

1. Extend your arms forward in the direction in which you want to go and tuck your chin to your chest.
2. At the same time, bend at your waist and push your chest down toward the bottom of the water.
3. This motion brings your hips to the surface, and you can push your chin forward until you are in a horizontal swimming position while taking your first stroke.

DRILLS FOR FEETFIRST ENTRY

Feetfirst entry is always the safest way to go, even when you can see the bottom or know the water depth. The advantages of this entry include keeping your head near the surface, or even above the water, if necessary due to cold or dirty conditions, for example, or to keep an eye on a target in the water.

Entry and Start Drill 1   Compact-Jump Entry and Swim

This drill helps you learn to get into the water from a dock or boat and immediately begin swimming. The object of the drill is to keep your body close to the surface and get to a horizontal position quickly and effectively. The drill requires you to find progressively shallower parts of the pool, down to 3.5 feet (~1 m). Find a suitable pool or body of water, check for any obstructions, and make sure that the conditions are safe.

To do the drill, perform the entry as described earlier. Standing on the side of the pool (or dock or boat), face the direction in which you are going to swim. Jump out away from the side and draw up your knees so that your legs are bent and your feet are under your hips. Extend your arms to your sides while in the air. As you hit the water, sweep your arms forward to absorb the energy from the drop and to keep your head above or near the surface of the water. Push your chest forward and kick your feet to the surface as quickly as possible.

TO INCREASE DIFFICULTY

- Try it from a block or diving board.

TO DECREASE DIFFICULTY

- Start from the side of the pool deck because it will be closer to the surface of the water than a boat deck or dock.

Success Check

- You can enter water that is 3.5 feet (~1 m) deep without touching the bottom with your feet.
- You can enter the water feetfirst and move 5 yards away from your entry point in three strokes.
- You can keep your head from completely submerging during the entry.

Score Your Success

1 point: You can do the drill from the entry.

3 points: You can do the drill and keep your head above water.

5 points: You can do the drill, keep your head above water, and move 5 yards in three strokes.

Entry and Start Drill 2 Stride-Jump Entry and Swim

Like the preceding drill, this one helps you learn to get into the water from a dock or boat and immediately begin swimming. Again, the object of the drill is to keep your body close to the surface and get to a horizontal position quickly and effectively. And again, the drill requires you to find progressively shallower parts of the pool, down to 3.5 feet (~1 m). The difference here is that you stride into the water with your legs separated rather than together.

After checking the water to ensure safe conditions, stand on the side of the pool (or dock or boat) and face the direction in which you are going to swim. Jump out away from the side and draw your knees up so that your legs are bent with one forward and one back, as if using a running stride. Extend your arms to your sides while in the air. As you enter, sweep your arms forward to prevent any further forward motion and to keep your head above water. Push your chest forward and kick your feet to the surface as quickly as possible. Begin swimming.

TO INCREASE DIFFICULTY

- Try it from a block or diving board.

TO DECREASE DIFFICULTY

- Start from the side of the pool deck because it will be closer to the surface of the water than a boat deck or dock.

Success Check

- You can enter water that is 3.5 feet (~1 m) deep without touching the bottom with your feet.
- You can enter the water feetfirst and move 5 yards away from your entry point in three strokes.
- You can keep your head from completing submerging during the entry.

Score Your Success

1 point: You can do the drill from the entry.

3 points: You can do the drill and keep your head above water.

5 points: You can do the drill, keep your head above water, and go 5 yards in three strokes.

Entry and Start Drill 3   Treading-Water Start

Many people have a natural ability to tread water, and there are many ways to tread effectively. The most common way is to use a horizontal sculling motion with the hands while breaststroke-kicking with one leg at a time. This kick is commonly referred to as the eggbeater. People who struggle with the breaststroke kick can use a version of the flutter kick just as effectively. Either of these kicks can be used for this drill.

The drill helps you prepare for times when you are stationary in the water and cannot push off of the bottom to get started. To do the drill, perform a sculling action with your hands in front to keep yourself stationary, then kick your legs and hips up to the surface. You must arch your back to keep your head out of the water, but once you are ready to go, just put your face in and start swimming.

Find a pool of sufficient depth that has plenty of room to execute the skill. Jump in feetfirst and begin treading. From the treading position, slowly bring your feet to the surface behind you with a kicking motion. To maintain balance, bring your sculling hands forward and continuing the sculling out front. Once you are horizontal, hold the position for at least a three-second count. Put your face in the water and begin swimming.

TO INCREASE DIFFICULTY

- Jump in from the deck, then get to a horizontal position as quickly as possible.

TO DECREASE DIFFICULTY

- Have a friend hold up your feet.

Success Check

- You can start horizontal and go 5 yards in three strokes.
- You can go from vertical treading to horizontal easily and quickly (in less than three seconds).
- You can keep your head from being submerged while you are horizontal until the start.

Score Your Success

1 point: You can do the drill with help.

3 points: You can do the drill and go 5 yards in three strokes.

5 points: You can do the drill after jumping into deep water.

Entry and Start Drill 4   Shore Entry and Dolphin-Dive Start

Use this drill when you enter from a beach or other shore with a shallow and long run out to deeper water. To do the drill, get clear knowledge of the bottom terrain, then wade into ankle-deep water. Continue wading out until the water is at least waist deep, then lean in, almost as if doing the butterfly stroke; be sure that your hands are in front of you before you push off of the bottom. Come up, stand, and repeat as necessary until you are in water of good swimming depth.

To do this drill in a pool, find a zero-entry pool or practice by diving over a lane line or noodle in shallow water. If you are in a zero-entry pool, be sure that it has sufficient depth for performing the drill safely. Keep your hands in front of your head when dolphining into the water so that any change in depth is felt by your hands—not your head. You can also dive under a lane line or noodle as if it were a wave coming in to the shore; swimming over such waves is a waste of energy, so it is better to simply duck under them.

TO INCREASE DIFFICULTY

- Push with one foot while maintaining forward movement with your other leg, as if you were striding on land.

TO DECREASE DIFFICULTY

- Stop after each dolphin.

Success Check

- You can dolphin-dive multiple times and transition to swimming.
- You can do multiple dolphins without pushing off of the bottom with your hands.
- You can perform the drill going both into and out of the water—that is, from shallow to deep and from deep to shallow.

Score Your Success

1 point: You can do the drill once.

3 points: You can do the drill three or more times in a row.

5 points: You can do the drill multiple times without pushing off of the bottom with your hands.

NAVIGATION AND SIGHTING

Since there is no pool marking for you to follow on the bottom of an open body of water, it is very helpful to develop skills that allow you to orient yourself in the water. Moreover, much of the world's open water provides you with only a few feet of visibility (if that), which limits the value of lifting your head for vision, especially since doing so can compromise your body position. In addition, without the benefit of a pool marking, most swimmers tend to pull to one side or the other, thus compounding the problem of navigation and encouraging you to look up more often than you need to.

Combine these factors with challenging wind, waves, or currents and you can end up all over the place. To make matters worse, the buoys that mark open-water courses are often are hard to see. In many cases, therefore, it is better to find a more prominent landmark on an opposite shore or some other stationary object to assure you that you are swimming straight (figure 9.4). Here are a few skills and drills to help you ensure that you swim in the right direction.

Figure 9.4   In open-water swimming, it's best to use a prominent landmark when sighting and navigating.

PREPARATION

1. Find a pool with an open lane that measures at least 25 yards.
2. At one end of the pool, stand directly on top of the lane stripe.

EXECUTION

1. Begin swimming freestyle and go for 10 strokes (each arm movement counts as one stroke) with your eyes closed.

2. Stop after 10 strokes and put your feet down. If you are still directly on top of the line, then you probably swim fairly straight and do not need to sight as much as some swimmers do.

3. If, on the other hand, you were bouncing off of the lane line to one side or the other, depending on overcorrections, you may want to review the freestyle step to adjust this pulling to one side and sight more frequently.

MISSTEP

You are exhausted after 25 yards of swimming.

CORRECTION

You are probably sighting too often. Doing so causes you to start and stop, which takes more energy. Sight a little less often.

MISSTEP

You end up way off course.

CORRECTION

Switch up your strokes and make sure that you are on line the whole way. This allows your muscles to recover slightly for at least one stroke. Perhaps sight a little more frequently and compensate if you find yourself tending to pull to one side.

SWITCH DRILLS

The following drills help you not only with sighting during a competition but also with engaging various muscles in a survival situation. The key in both cases is to perform the skills with minimal energy expenditure.

Switch Drill 1   Freestyle-to-Breaststroke Switch

As mentioned in step 5, the breaststroke is the slowest of the competitive strokes but offers some advantages. Aside from getting to breathe on every stroke, you also get to look forward, which of course is very helpful when you need to quickly check where you're going while continuing to make progress. In short, the breaststroke allows you to simultaneously get a peek—for example, at a buoy or landmark—and a little air. To perform this drill, swim seven strokes of freestyle followed by three strokes of breaststroke and then go back to freestyle.

TO INCREASE DIFFICULTY

- Swim multiple cycles of the drill.

TO DECREASE DIFFICULTY

- Stop after each switch.

Success Check

- You can do the drill with a switch to breaststroke and a switch back to freestyle.
- You can do multiple cycles of the drill.
- You can do multiple cycles of the drill without stopping.

Score Your Success

1 point: You can do the drill once.

3 points: You can do the drill three or more times in a row.

5 points: You can do the drill multiple times with no hesitation.

Switch Drill 2   Freestyle-to-Backstroke Switch

There are also advantages to switching from freestyle to backstroke. First, you get to breathe for a bit with your face out of the water so that you can also clear your goggles or rest tired muscles used in the freestyle. Second, you can sneak a look back and see where you have been to track progress and check heading.

To perform this drill, swim seven strokes of freestyle, then roll over and swim three strokes of backstroke before returning to freestyle. During one of the freestyle strokes it is okay to lift your head to see your competition or (in competition or survival situations) to see where you have been in order to judge the current.

TO INCREASE DIFFICULTY

• Swim multiple cycles of the drill.

TO DECREASE DIFFICULTY

• Stop after each switch.

Success Check

• You can do the drill with a switch to backstroke and a switch back to freestyle.
• You can do multiple cycles of the drill.
• You can do multiple cycles of the drill without stopping.

Score Your Success

1 point: You can do the drill once.

3 points: You can do the drill three or more times in a row.

5 points: You can do the drill multiple times with no hesitation.

Switch Drill 3   Surfing the Goggles

This is a great drill for mastering freestyle in flatter water. To perform it, simply press down slightly during the catch so that only your goggles break the surface, thus allowing you to get a quick peek. The breath is still taken in a separate movement from the peek to the side. The drill allows you to figure out the best height for your goggles and find your rhythm.

First, take three strokes and then lift your head completely out of the water, making sure that even your chin comes out. Repeat this sequence for 25 yards. Now do the drill again but this time lift your head until just your mouth and nose are out of the water. Then try it with just your goggles coming out. You should notice that surfing just the goggles is easier and prevents you from stopping in the water. In each iteration, after you take your sighting, press your chest down to regain horizontal equilibrium and avoid having to kick your way back to horizontal. This undulating motion also maintains your momentum.

How often do you need to look? You should have a pretty good idea of your answer to this question if you did the eyes-closed exercise for navigation and sighting described earlier. Try it some more to make sure that you know what works best for you.

TO INCREASE DIFFICULTY

- Swim multiple cycles of the drill without stopping.

<table>
<tr><td>

Success Check

- You can do the drill in all three positions
- You can do multiple cycles of the drill.
- You can do multiple cycles of the drill without stopping.

</td><td>

Score Your Success

1 point: You can do the drill once.

3 points: You can do the drill three or more times in a row.

5 points: You can do the drill multiple times with no hesitation.

</td></tr>
</table>

PACK SWIMMING

One of the most useful tools in an open-water swim is the ability to draft. Pack swimming (figure 9.5) involves a lot of contact and often leaves very little space in the water for just you. As in cycling, the pack moves as a group, and everyone tries to find the right spot in which to gain an advantage. Also as in cycling, drafting gives swimmers a little extra lift and makes the work a bit easier. Another benefit is that you get to let someone else navigate—assuming he or she swims straight!

Unlike in cycling, the ideal swimming draft is done to the side and back rather than directly behind. To get the idea, think of how geese fly. Aim to have your head somewhere between the lead swimmer's hip and her or his ankle; the exact positioning depends on the swimmer's size, shape, velocity, and swim conditions.

Figure 9.5   When swimming in a pack, you will come into contact with other swimmers, so it's important to learn how to draft.

To perform this technique, you and a friend or instructor both leave the wall, the friend or instructor leaving first. Find the spot where your freestyle stroke is long and smooth as described in the positioning previously. In the boundary layer between fluids and other materials, the velocities shed by and object provide vectors of force in a variety of directions. If you can minimize the energy while maintaining a velocity by making your strokes long and smooth, then you have found a good drafting position. Try both the right and left sides until you determine which one you like best.

PREPARATION

1. Find two swimmers to help you with this skill.
2. Make sure that you have a free lane in which to practice the skill.
3. Ensure that no swimmers are coming the other way.

EXECUTION

1. Have the first swimmer start by swimming down the center of the lane.
2. After waiting a second or two, the second and third swimmers can start at the same time on either side.
3. The draft position is slightly to the side, much like geese use when flying in an echelon formation.
4. The best draft position is with the head somewhere between the lead swimmer's hip and ankle.
5. Adjust your draft position forward and backward in this zone until you can feel the benefit of the draft.

MISSTEP
You end up getting splashed in the face and constantly swallow water.

CORRECTION
Switch sides.

MISSTEP
You get kicked in the face by the lead swimmer.

CORRECTION
You are out of position and should move up and off to the side a bit rather than following right behind the lead swimmer.

DRILLS FOR PACK SWIMMING

Drafting is more subtle in swimming than in cycling or auto racing. The positioning differs as well. In cycling and auto racing, the ideal draft position is often behind the lead cyclist or driver, but this is not true of swimming. In swimming, the swimmers can be off to the side. To practice your position and drafting skills, use the following drills.

Pack-Swimming Drill 1   Three-Person Drafting

In a 25-yard pool, work with two other swimmers. Start one right after another and have the second and third swimmers get into drafting position. Switch lead swimmers every 25 yards. You can use either a V formation with a drafter on either side of the lead swimmer or a diagonal formation in which swimmer 2 drafts off of the lead swimmer and swimmer 3 drafts off of swimmer 2.

TO INCREASE DIFFICULTY

- Swim at least 75 yards without stopping.

TO DECREASE DIFFICULTY

- Stop after each 25 yards.
- Wear fins.

Success Check

- You can do the drill with all three swimmers taking a turn as leader.
- You can do multiple cycles of the drill.
- You can do multiple cycles of the drill without stopping.

Score Your Success

1 point: You can do the drill once while drafting.

3 points: You can do the drill once while leading.

5 points: You can do the drill multiple times from any position.

Pack-Swimming Drill 2   Rollover

This drill is helpful if you like drafting on one side better than on the other because it helps you learn to switch from one side of the lead swimmer to the other side. To perform the drill, start by rolling inward and taking one backstroke stroke in a twisting motion. As your backstroke arm reaches for the catch, your body width matches that of the lead swimmer, and after completing the roll, your next stroke is on the opposite side. In other words, depending on which side you start on, you either do a backstroke with your left hand and roll to the front with a right-hand stroke, or vice versa.

This maneuver puts you on the other side of the lead swimmer's feet without losing momentum. It is a little tricky, and you should practice it in a pool before trying it in an open-water environment.

TO INCREASE DIFFICULTY

- Swim at least 75 yards without stopping.

TO DECREASE DIFFICULTY

- Stop after each 25 yards.
- Wear fins.

Success Check

- You can do the drill with all three leaders.
- You can do multiple cycles of the drill.
- You can do multiple cycles of the drill without stopping.

Score Your Success

1 point: You can do the drill once.

3 points: You can do the drill from either side.

5 points: You can do the drill multiple times from either side.

CHANGING DIRECTION

Most open-water swims require you to turn or at least change direction. Doing so without losing momentum is an art form. When swimming freestyle, the human body is just not meant to bend laterally very much; humans are much better at bending forward at the waist. Having said that, one of the more effective turns involves taking one backstroke stroke and bending at the waist so that your upper body points in the direction in which you want to go after the turn. Your legs will follow. This technique allows you to change direction without breaking rhythm, and swimmers who can touch their toes can use it to make as much as a 180-degree direction change.

Another effective turn is the one-arm turn, which is a little more conservative and flat. To perform it, extend your inside arm in front of you and position the palm of that hand vertically so that it acts like a rudder. Use your other arm to stroke until you finish the turn. Your inside arm is closer to the buoy, and your stroking arm is farther from it.

Follow these steps to practice changing directions.

PREPARATION

1. Find a wide part of the pool.
2. Use a makeshift buoy (e.g., a balloon anchored to the bottom) or have a fellow swimmer stand in shallower water to act as a buoy.

EXECUTION

1. Start at least 15 yards away from the buoy.
2. Begin swimming freestyle and sight the buoy at least once.
3. After reaching the buoy, bring your hands together out front.
4. With your inside arm extended, turn your hand to a vertical position.
5. Pont the fingers of that hand in the direction in which you want to go.
6. Stroke quickly with your opposite arm.
7. Once the turn is complete, continue swimming as usual.

MISSTEP

You have to stop at the buoy or turn around to go in the opposite direction.

CORRECTION

Remember that it takes more energy to get going again after stopping, so even if your turn is wide just keep swimming.

MISSTEP

You get squeezed out of a turn by a leading swimmer.

CORRECTION

Switch sides on the turn or duck under.

DRILLS FOR THE TURN

Because our bodies have a harder time bending laterally, staying flat without any assistance makes for a very wide turn. The following drills help you learn the skills necessary to corner with the greatest efficiency.

Turn Drill 1   Rollover Turn

This is an excellent drill for working on your cornering. In either a shallow or deep end with no lane lines, have a partner stand or tread water to act as a buoy; alternatively, if you can remove the lane lines, simply use a simple balloon anchored to the bottom by a weight. Make sure to leave sufficient room for the turn. Roll onto your back, from your outside arm inward, to facilitate the bend at the waist and perform one backstroke pull. Practice this skill for both right and left turns.

TO INCREASE DIFFICULTY

- Swim around the buoy in one direction, then immediately repeat in the other direction.
- Turn greater than 90 degrees.

TO DECREASE DIFFICULTY

- Stop after each turn.
- Wear fins.

Success Check

- You can do the turn to both the right and left sides.
- You can do the turn without breaking rhythm.
- You can do the turn multiple times with ease and without breaking rhythm.

Score Your Success

1 point: You can do the drill once to one side.

3 points: You can do the drill once to either side.

5 points: You can do the drill multiple times to either side.

Turn Drill 2   One-Arm Turn

This drill works on a turn that is effective for getting around a buoy when you need to sight the whole time or are uncomfortable with the rollover drill. In either a shallow or deep end with no lane lines, have a partner stand or tread water to act as the buoy; alternatively, if you can remove the lane lines, simply use a balloon anchored to the bottom by a weight. Use your lead arm and hand (inside, closest to the buoy) as a rudder and steer yourself around the buoy while using your other arm to stroke. Practice this skill for both right and left turns.

TO INCREASE DIFFICULTY

- Swim around the buoy in one direction, then immediately repeat in the other direction.

TO DECREASE DIFFICULTY

- Stop after each turn.
- Wear fins.

Success Check

- You can do the turn to both the right and left sides.
- You can do the turn without breaking rhythm.
- You can do the turn multiple times with ease and without breaking rhythm.

Score Your Success

1 point: You can do the drill once to one side.

3 points: You can do the drill once to either side.

5 points: You can do the drill multiple times to either side.

FINISH AND EXIT

Whether you are finishing and exiting a race or swimming in a survival situation, it is critical to conserve energy. Swimmers who are accustomed to using an energy-conserving two-beat kick often find that the body directs all of its energy resources to the muscles doing the most work in the upper body. For this reason, competitive open-water swimmers and triathletes alike often experience cramping in the lower body and a lack of balance upon getting back on dry land. With this risk in mind, it is important to get circulation and resources flowing to the lower body as well—regardless of how you get out of the water, you will need to use your legs to walk or run.

Another hazard arises for many competitive swimmers and triathletes after they round the final buoy. At this point, they make a mad dash for the shore without thinking much about sighting, which may cause them to waste energy by swimming too far due to poor navigation. It is also important at this stage to maintain rhythm to prevent swimming too far or going into oxygen debt before the end of the race, forcing you to back off the pace.

EXITING THE WATER

Exits will vary depending on the course some are ramp exits while others are just shore approaches. The exit is similar to the entry in a few ways. The first is that you have to make sure you have a target to reach. Knowing where the finish is and about what the distance from the last turn is will be helpful here.

Next is the fact that kicking is important. In the beginning of an open water race, many swimmers use a high kick tempo to create separation from the pack. Afterwards, they may settle into a slower two- or four-beat kick to save energy. The problem with this is that much of the body's resources get concentrated in the upper body as the legs do not require as much. It is important to remember to pick up the kick to increase the blood flow to the lower extremities.

MISSTEP

You run up onto the beach and immediately experience leg cramps.

CORRECTION

Make sure to kick your legs to get more blood circulating back into them during the last part of the swim.

MISSTEP

You have to stop before getting to the exit in order to locate it.

CORRECTION

Make sure that you are on line by sighting a few times at the last turn and a few more times on the way in.

DRILL FOR EXITING THE WATER

Depending on the approach it may be helpful to do a few dolphin dives (figure 9.6) as the water gets a little shallower but still too deep to effectively run. This is the same skill as the entry portion only you will dolphin dive first then run when shallow.

Figure 9.6 Dolphin dive.

Open-Water Exit Drill   Dolphin Dive Exit

As with the dolphin dive entry, you can use this technique when you exit the beach or other shore with a shallow and long run up from deeper water.

Once you start swimming toward water that is shallow enough to touch bottom, continue swimming into shore until the water is at most thigh deep. Lean in, almost as if doing the butterfly stroke. Make sure that your hands are in front of you before you push off of the bottom. Come up, stand, and repeat as necessary until you are in shallow enough water that you can stand up and walk easily.

TO INCREASE DIFFICULTY

- Push with one foot while maintaining forward movement with your other leg.

TO DECREASE DIFFICULTY

- Stop after each dolphin.

Success Check

- You can dolphin-dive multiple times and transition to running.
- You can do multiple dolphins without pushing off of the bottom with your hands.
- You can perform the drill going both into and out of the water.

Score Your Success

1 point: You can do the drill once.

3 points: You can do the drill three or more times in a row.

5 points: You can do the drill multiple times without pushing off of the bottom with your hands.

SURVIVAL SWIMMING

Sidestroke, though not a competitive stroke, is a great stroke to master for open-water and survival swimming. It allows you to have your face out of the water to breathe and uses a powerful scissorlike kick. Like breaststroke, it derives propulsion almost equally from armstroking and kicking. As the name implies, sidestroke is done on the side; one shoulder and arm are toward the bottom of the pool, and the other shoulder is out of the water with the majority of the arm submerged. As with the other strokes discussed in this book, the best way to master the sidestroke is to master its individual elements separately and then put them all together.

Sidestroke Kicking

The sidestroke employs a scissor kick (figure 9.7), which differs from the flutter kick in that the legs are wide apart and the swimmer is on his or her side. To perform the scissor kick, bring the leg that is closer to the surface forward by drawing the knee toward your chest. The leg that is closer to the bottom of the pool extends back so that you are almost in a stridelike position on your side. Next, bring your legs together while extending the leg that was drawn to the chest. As you wedge yourself forward, you should feel the pressure on the back of your top leg and on the front of your bottom leg.

Figure 9.7 SIDESTROKE KICK

Preparation

1. Ensure that you have adequate space to do the stroke.
2. Get in the water and lie on your front in the neutr al position.

Execution

1. With one arm extended, rotate to the side and sweep your other arm down so that it is closest to the top of the water and your face is turned out of the water.
2. Bring your feet wide in a scissorlike fashion and sweep them together.
3. After you glide for a second or two, repeat the kick in that same position.

MISSTEP
You keep both legs straight and just move them back and forth.

CORRECTION
Both knees need to bend as you separate into a stridelike position. The force of the movement needs to be backward in order to provide a propulsive forward movement.

MISSTEP
You bring your upper leg back and your lower leg forward.

CORRECTION
This will work to a small extent, but you will tend to roll over on your back. Make sure to bring your upper leg forward.

Sidestroke Arm Sweep

Armstroking in the sidestroke (figure 9.8) involves a chain of movements. The extended arm sweeps down, with the elbow bent, to about the mid body; whereas the arm closest to the surface sneaks up along the body. The hands meet, and the arm closest to the surface then pushes back down toward the thigh while the other arm sneaks forward. Many swimmers benefit from using the mental image of reaching to pick an apple, then transferring it to the other hand to put it in a bag at the hip.

Figure 9.8 **SIDESTROKE ARM SWEEP**

Preparation

1. Make sure that you have adequate space to do the stroke.
2. Get in the water and lie on your front in the neutral position.

Execution

1. With the one arm extended, rotate to the side and sweep your other arm down so that it is closer to the top of the water and your face is turned out of the water.
2. Pull the arm that is closer to the bottom of the water toward your chest in a sweeping motion.
3. At the same time, sneak your upper arm and hand forward to meet your bottom arm.
4. As your hands touch, turn the hand of your upper arm to put pressure on the water down to your side.
5. As you do so, sneak your bottom arm forward to the starting position.
6. Repeat.

MISSTEP

You keep splashing at the water with your lead hand.

CORRECTION

Remember to slide the hand forward rather than reach over the water.

MISSTEP

You push your lead hand down rather than back to lift your head.

CORRECTION

This is a common temptation as a way to get the head higher; remember, however, to lay your head on your lead arm and then sweep back.

Complete Sidestroke

The process of putting it all together for the sidestroke is very similar to the process for the breaststroke in that your arm and leg movements must be somewhat independent. The most effective use of the powerful kick is to perform it while you are extended, with your lead arm out, so be patient. While your legs recover to kick again, your momentum should be maintained by the propulsive force of the pull and armstroke. Do the following to practice the complete sidestroke.

PREPARATION

1. Make sure that you have adequate space to do the stroke.
2. Get into the water and lie on your front in the neutral position.

EXECUTION

1. With the one arm extended, rotate to the side and sweep your other arm down so that it is closer to the top of the water and your face is turned out of the water.
2. Bring your feet wide in a scissorlike fashion and sweep them together.

3. After you glide for a second or two, pull the arm closest to the bottom of the pool toward your chest in a sweeping motion.

4. At the same time, sneak your upper arm and hand forward to meet your bottom arm.

5. As your hands touch, turn the hand of your upper arm to put pressure on the water down to your side.

6. As you do so, sneak your bottom arm forward to the starting position.

7. Repeat by beginning again with the kick after returning.

MISSTEP
You claw at the water while kicking.

CORRECTION
Remember to slide your hand forward first, then kick and glide.

MISSTEP
You pull and kick at the same time and keep sinking.

CORRECTION
Lay your head on your lead arm and kick. Exhale slowly and glide. Roll your face to air, then pull and kick again.

ELEMENTARY BACKSTROKE

Though not a competitive stroke, the elementary backstroke (figure 9.9) is an effective open-water tool and a great stroke for survival swimming because it enables you to propel yourself while expending minimal energy. In addition, your face is always out of the water, which enables you to breathe easily. The stroke is performed by incorporating an arm push and a breaststroke kick while lying on your back. Unlike the breaststroke, this stroke involves nearly simultaneous arm and leg movements. Make sure that your arms stay in the water the whole time. When practicing this stroke in a pool, make sure that the backstroke flags are in place or have a friend observe to prevent you from running into the wall.

Figure 9.9 **ELEMENTARY BACKSTROKE**

Preparation

1. Make sure that you have room to do the skill.
2. Ensure that the backstroke flags are in place or have a friend observe to prevent you from hitting your head.

Execution

1. As in the breaststroke, each movement in this stroke is separate. Begin by floating on your back.
2. Draw your arms up with your hands in close at your sides.

3. When your elbows are in line with your shoulders, sweep your hands out with your palms down.
4. From the T position, rotate your palms to vertical and sweep your hands down to your sides.
5. Bring your heels up while gliding from this motion, then point your toes out as in the breaststroke.
6. Grab the water with your insteps and sweep your feet together.
7. As you finish the kick, begin another arm cycle.
8. If you not proficient in the breaststroke kick, you can substitute the flutter kick.

MISSTEP

You push down with your hands rather than laterally toward your thighs.

CORRECTION

This motion causes you to "bounce" in the water and likely makes your face sink when you recover your hands. Be sure to push in a sweeping motion toward your thighs.

MISSTEP

You kick out with your legs and draw your knees up too high.

CORRECTION

This motion causes water to rush up to your face and provides you with little or no propulsion. Instead, make sure to push your lower legs together with the inside of your calves and your insteps.

SWIM, FLOAT, AND SWIM AGAIN

This strategy gives you a simple way to prevent exhaustion if you are intentionally swimming a long distance or become tired in an emergency situation. It consists simply of swimming one of the strokes you have learned in the previous steps, then rolling onto your back and floating in the neutral position to rest. You then roll back over and continue swimming. When fatigue returns, repeat the process.

To practice this sequence, swim until you feel tired, then roll over to float (figure 9.10). Once you have recovered, continue swimming. Performing this skill multiple times over several hundred yards will increase your confidence in open water.

Figure 9.10 PROPER FLOATING TECHNIQUE

Preparation

1. Make sure that you have adequate space to perform the skill.
2. Make sure that you are the only one in your lane and that no swimmers are coming in the other direction.

Execution

1. Begin at the end of the lane and swim freestyle (or breast-stroke or sidestroke) for seven strokes.
2. Roll onto your back and assume a neutral back-float position as described in steps 1 and 2.
3. Rest comfortably on the water for 5 to 10 seconds.
4. Reach over your body with one of your arms and resume swimming as usual.
5. Repeat as often as necessary to become comfortable with the sequence.

MISSTEP

You swim until tired and then tread water.

CORRECTION

This approach can be somewhat effective but provides less rest because treading is an active water skill.

DRILLS FOR SURVIVAL SWIMMING

Survival swimming is much like any other kind of swimming in the sense that it is a specific skillset that when practiced and mastered cannot only add to the enjoyment of swimming but also potentially save your life. The following drills are meant to enhance your ability to perform each skill with as little effort as possible to conserve energy in an emergency situation.

Survival Swimming Drill 1   Scissor Kick With Kickboard

While lying on your side in the water, lay the kickboard on the water with one arm extended on the board and your other arm at your side. Practice the scissor kick multiple times with your head on your extended arm and the board. Try this drill on both the right and the left sides; you will probably find one side easier than the other.

TO INCREASE DIFFICULTY

- Hold the kickboard with just your hand rather than having your whole arm on the board.

TO DECREASE DIFFICULTY

- Have a friend or coach hold your hips up for the first few tries.

Success Check

- You can keep your hips vertical.
- You can do a long glide after each kick.

Score Your Success

1 point: You can do the drill for 15 yards on one side.

3 points: You can do the drill 25 yards on one side.

5 points: You can do the drill on either side for 25 yards.

Survival Swimming Drill 2 Tennis Ball

To perform this partner drill, get into shallow water and extend into the sidestroke position. Now, have a partner hand you a tennis ball that you transfer from your lead hand to your lower hand. After releasing the ball, repeat the sequence with another ball, and so on. You will need approximately four to five tennis balls. It is best to do this drill with a pull buoy for support, but kicking is also okay.

TO INCREASE DIFFICULTY

- Use a smaller item, such as a table tennis ball.

TO DECREASE DIFFICULTY

- Have a friend or coach hold your hips up for the first few tries.

Success Check

- You can keep your hips vertical.
- You can do the drill without missing a ball.

Score Your Success

1 point: You can do the drill for 15 yards on one side.

3 points: You can do the drill 25 yards on one side.

5 points: You can do the drill on either side for 25 yards.

Survival Swimming Drill 3 Ride the Glide

This drill helps you with timing and with putting it all together. To do the drill, perform one kick, stretch as far forward as possible with your lead arm, and glide until you stop. At this point, perform one armstroke to recover your legs and move forward. Repeat for a total of five kicks.

TO INCREASE DIFFICULTY

- Try the drill on both sides.

TO DECREASE DIFFICULTY

- Use fins.

Success Check

- You can keep your hips vertical.
- You can do the drill while keeping your head at the surface of the water.

Score Your Success

1 point: You can go 15 yards with five kicks.

3 points: You can go 20 yards with five kicks.

5 points: You can go 25 yards with five kicks.

Survival Swimming Drill 4   Arms Only

This is a great drill for getting used to the arm movement of the elementary backstroke. To do the drill, get a pull buoy to help keep your lower body up while you focus on the arm movements. Complete one full stroke, then glide and let yourself come to a complete stop. Repeat five times and see how far you can go.

TO INCREASE DIFFICULTY

- Try the drill with no pull buoy and no kicking.

TO DECREASE DIFFICULTY

- Use more than one pull buoy.

Success Check

- You can stay faceup and flat on the water.
- You can do the drill while keeping your head, chest, hips, and feet all at the surface.

Score Your Success

1 point: You can go 15 yards with five pulls.

3 points: You can go 20 yards with five pulls.

5 points: You can go 25 yards with five pulls.

Survival Swimming Drill 5   Swim, Float, Swim

This drill gives you an effective way to practice long-distance swimming. To do it, swim at least 75 yards of freestyle, then turn over and float for 20 seconds. Roll back over and swim at least 75 yards of breaststroke, then roll over again and rest for another 20 seconds. Repeat again with freestyle and continue this pattern until you have swum a total of 450 yards or more!

TO INCREASE DIFFICULTY

- Try the drill with just freestyle swimming and floating.

TO DECREASE DIFFICULTY

- Incorporate additional types of stroke (e.g., elementary backstroke).

Success Check

- You can remain faceup and flat on the water.
- You can do the full sequence—switching from stroke to float and back to stroke—with ease.

Score Your Success

1 point: You can go 225 yards.

3 points: You can go 300 yards.

5 points: You can go 450 yards.

SUCCESS SUMMARY

Swimming in open water resembles pool swimming in important ways but also involves additional skills that make it very different in some respects. Environmental concerns and the lack of control over many elements of the swimming venue make open-water swimming particularly challenging; they also elevate the need for caution and close attention to safety.

SCORE YOUR SUCCESS

If you scored at least 45 points, then you have completed this step. If you scored 46 to 60 points, then you are well on your way and have the potential to enjoy open-water swimming for recreation. If you scored more than 60 points, then you have mastered the key elements for taking your swimming to the next level.

Entry and Start Drills

1. Compact-Jump Entry and Swim	___ out of 5
2. Stride-Jump Entry and Swim	___ out of 5
3. Treading-Water Start	___ out of 5
4. Shore Entry and Dolphin-Dive Start	___ out of 5

Switch Drills

1. Freestyle-to-Breaststroke Switch	___ out of 5
2. Freestyle-to-Backstroke Switch	___ out of 5
3. Surfing the Goggles	___ out of 5

Pack-Swimming Drills

1. Three-Person Drafting	___ out of 5
2. Rollover	___ out of 5

Turn Drills

1. Rollover Turn	___ out of 5
2. One-Arm Turn	___ out of 5

Open-Water Exit Drill

1. Dolphin Dive Exit	___ out of 5

Survival Swimming Drills

1. Scissor Kick Drill With Kickboard	___ out of 5
2. Tennis Ball	___ out of 5
3. Ride the Glide	___ out of 5
4. Arms Only	___ out of 5
5. Swim, Float, Swim	___ out of 5
Total	**___ out of 85**

Continuing With Swimming

Y ou have now taken the first steps in your swimming journey. If you have found greater confidence in the water as you have progressed through the steps in this book, it is time to explore options for continuing your swimming, whether for recreation or for competition.

The first part of the process involves finding a place to swim regularly. Many parks and recreation departments maintain swimming pools that are open to the public on at least a seasonal basis. Other places to search include the YMCA, YWCA, Jewish Community Centers, fitness clubs, swim clubs, schools, and health and wellness centers. Key considerations include schedule, quality of facilities, staff, and, of course, cost.

The next part of the process involves practicing the skills that you have already mastered and building on them. The sport of swimming depends on skill-based movement, and it is often helpful to go all the way back to the beginning to review what you have done and see where you can make improvements. Now that you have been through the process once—and gained a new level of confidence in the water—it would be a good idea to go back through the steps and make sure that you get them right at the highest level of which you are capable.

GOAL SETTING

Goal setting is an important part of any healthy lifestyle, whether it is done for fitness, recreation, or competition. Regardless of what area of life you are addressing, goal setting gives you direction and focus. It helps shape your decision making, not just about how you spend your exercise time but also about other aspects of your life, such as what you eat and drink and how much rest you get.

If you are interested in swimming purely as a way to stay fit or get fit, then you may think that goal setting is unimportant in this area of your life. That is, however, far from true. Fitness goals do tend to take on different characteristics than competitive goals, but they are goals nonetheless. Here are just a few examples of fitness goals: lowering your heart rate, losing weight, feeling better, making your clothes fit better, and cross-training.

Swimming is also used by athletes from other sports who want to supplement their usual routine or rehab an injury. In fact, there is a whole branch of sports medicine and rehab that use aquatics as a way of getting people back into athletics—or just back into their normal pattern of life. In addition, more and more physicians are prescribing exercise as a pathway to better health on all levels.

For recreational swimmers, goals are a little easier to quantify, since they often involve either distance or time or both. Many recreational swimmers are also seeking to do a first triathlon or perhaps just become able to swim a certain distance or swim for a certain amount of time. These swimmers need to set a goal to get them out of bed for a morning workout or help them be sure to swing by the pool on the way home from work. In other examples, a person might set a goal of obtaining scuba certification or getting fit enough to keep up with active peers. Swimmers in this category also set goals for becoming more comfortable in the water and more efficient in their movements.

If you have found that you excel in a given stroke, then you may wish to think about competing. Competitive goals tend to be tightly focused, and they vary widely from swimmer to swimmer. For example, some swimmers aim to do better in the swim portion of a local triathlon, whereas others want to compete in open-water or pool-based events. The best and most focused goals are based on measurable criteria, such as performing a specific stroke for a specific time and distance. This type of goal is much different from, say, setting a general goal of winning.

How to Do It Well

Regardless of whether you are a fitness, recreational, or competitive swimmer, your goals should be challenging and motivating. Many people have found that they set more effective goals if they use a system based on the acronym SMART.

The S in SMART stands for *specific*, which means that the goal should include meaningful detail about activity, time, location, and requirements. A vague goal might read like this: "I am going to start swimming more." In contrast, a more specific goal might read like this: "I am going to swim three or more times per week." This kind of specificity is useful in fitness, recreational, and competitive swimming.

The M in SMART stands for *measurable*. Setting measurable goals helps you hold yourself accountable and motivates you when you reach milestones by giving you a sense of accomplishment. The key here is to determine what you are trying to measure. For example, a fitness swimmer might track number of swims, a recreational swimmer might track distance covered, and a competitive swimmer might track times.

The A stands for *achievable*. It may be inspirational to think that you can do anything you set your mind to, but it is often more effective to set short-term goals that are attainable on your way to achieving a long-term ambition. Achievable goals serve as milestones on your path to a bigger goal. The best part is that the more often you achieve meaningful goals, the better you get at developing the skills, personal attributes, mind-set, and habits that lead you to bigger goals.

The R stands for *realistic*. When setting goals, you should always be honest with yourself. For example, if you have just started swimming and have mastered all of the strokes presented in this book, then you might set a realistic goal of swimming a mile (1.6 km) without stopping within the next year. An example of an unrealistic goal would be trying to make the U.S. national swim team in the next six months. Granted, this is a dramatic example, but it can in fact be a tricky thing to set a realistic goal. Make it too easy and there is no challenge; a result, meeting your goals may ring hollow. Make it too challenging and you may get frustrated with the process and move on to something else.

Finally, the T stands for *time*—that is, identifying a specific time period in which you want to accomplish your goal. This is the part of your goal that gets you out of bed on a cold morning or motivates you to squeeze in a swim over lunch. You are typically happy later on for doing so, but many of us can rationalize many reasons to skip what we know is good for us in exchange for an extra 10 minutes of sleep or a slice of pizza or scoop of ice cream. Mind you, these things are not necessarily bad in their proper place, but a time-limited goal keeps your focus on what you want to achieve and when you want to get it done. Simply saying "I want to lose weight" has no real meaning in terms of time, but saying "I want to lose five pounds by January 1" puts the goal on the clock and is much more likely to change your behavior.

Following Up on Goals

Once you achieve a goal, what comes next? In competitive swimming, the answer is easy because the next goal can always be set by the clock. In contrast, fitness and recreational swimmers might focus on doing more frequent swims or even having a go at competitive swimming. Regardless of how you frame the issue, have your next goal ready when you achieve your current one. In addition, make time to celebrate your achievements. Reward and recognition are very motivating, especially when the rewards are intrinsic.

FINDING A PROGRAM

Various programs are available, and the right choice depends on your goals. For example, if you are a fitness or recreational swimmer, you may not need a lot of structure; in fact, you may find great satisfaction in accomplishing everything on your own. Due to the technical nature of the sport, however, most people need a support group or program to help them along. Many large metropolitan areas are home to a diverse group of swimming programs; smaller areas may have fewer options. In either case, certain questions can help you decide whether to join a program or continue on your own.

Two big considerations are program schedule and program structure. If the program's schedule does not fit yours, this need not necessarily be end of the conversation with that facility. Ask if the staff would consider offering a program at a time that works better for you. Many swimmers just accept a schedule as it is posted and move on if it doesn't work for them, but sometimes a facility manager is simply unaware of the demand for a different time slot. If a number of swimmers show up at the pool at the same time you prefer, go ahead and ask the management about starting a new offering or expanding an existing one.

The structure of the program is also a consideration. Some programs just have a workout leader who swims the workout and provides minimal feedback. Others are more instructive, providing a teacher in the water or on the deck who can give individual feedback and really help participants improve. Still other programs have a full-time professional coach on the deck who helps swimmers both with workout considerations and with stroke improvement. The most instructive setup, of course, is the lesson environment. A careful review of your experience with this book can help you identify what type of program is best suited to your needs and goals.

CHOOSING A COACH OR INSTRUCTOR

This process involves a number of factors, all of which focus on you; indeed, swimming programs exist not because of coaches or instructors but because of swimmers. As in any profession, there are good coaches and instructors, and there are poor ones. In addition, what works for one swimmer may not work for another. As much as possible, your choice should be dictated by your goals and your level of proficiency.

For any swimmer, the introduction to a program, coach, or instructor should always start with a conversation. If yours is a new face on the pool deck, then you can expect someone from the program to greet you. Hopefully, that person does a short interview and asks about your swimming background. The best bet is to be honest so that the coach or instructor gets a good idea of what you want and need.

It is also a good idea to ask him or her plenty of questions. Here are a few examples: What is your coaching philosophy? How do you integrate new people into the group? And what is the fee for the program? As for program content, some coaches and instructors take a workout-oriented approach, whereas others focus more on instruction. Neither approach is necessarily better than the other; again, it depends on your goals.

The nature of a good coach or instructor may vary from one person's opinion to another, but certain characteristics are shared by all great coaches in any sport. First, they care—not only about the sport and its highest-level athletes but also about helping every athlete they encounter, regardless of level or goals, to love the sport and continually seek improvement. They put effort into each athlete and each session while also working to make themselves better. This is what coaching grit is all about. If one method doesn't work, they try another—and another and another—until they are successful with each athlete. Nor are they afraid to ask for help from a colleague; in fact, the best coaches do this all the time. They are committed to helping athletes achieve their goals, which is why they are themselves successful. Where do you find these programs and people? Read on.

SWIMMING RESOURCES

The next part of your journey into the wider world of swimming is to look for resources to help you become a better swimmer. Of course, several resources are available from Human Kinetics that are part of the aquatics department. There are also multimedia resources, such as videos and other instructional media. A word of caution: Most anyone can "publish" most anything on the web, which means that you need to exercise a critical eye in selecting swimming materials. The most reputable sources for additional instruction are the national governing bodies that work with aquatics, from the very young to the most senior members of the aquatics community. Through these organizations, you can find numerous resources, including in-person coaching.

USA Swimming (www.usaswimming.org) is the governing body that regulates U.S. swimming for age groups from eight and under all the way through elite international competition, including the Olympics. USA Swimming is governed primarily by volunteers, and contact can be made through Local Swimming Committees (LSCs) since the organization is structured geographically. Simply access the USA Swimming website, which will put you in touch with local resources to help you along on your swimming journey if you are looking for a very high level of competition or access to coaches at this level.

U.S. Masters Swimming (www.usms.org) is dedicated to providing adults 18 years old and over with access to health, wellness, fitness, and competition through aquatics. Adults seeking resources (e.g., workout plans and additional instruction) can look here to find programs for aquatics at every level in their local area. Like USA Swimming, this organization depends on volunteers and operates in the same manner—in this case, through Local Masters Swimming Committees (LMSCs).

Another national governing body that deals with adult aquatics and fitness on a variety of levels in USA Triathlon (www.usatriathlon.org). This organization addresses all ages and, since one of the disciplines of triathlon is swimming, it can provide you with a number of opportunities to continue your swimming if you choose multisport racing for fitness or competition.

In addition to national governing bodies, there are a number of professional swim teaching and coaching organizations that you can contact for additional resources. All you need to do is search for them using keywords such as "swim instruction" or "swim lessons." Many can be found at the same facilities that you are looking at to secure lane space, so you have a convenient way to continue your journey.

Swimming is a great sport for health, wellness, and competition; it is also a life skill in that it can mean surviving an emergency situation. May this book not only help you be a better swimmer but also set you on the path to swimming as a lifelong sport!

About the Author

Scott Bay is an American Swimming Coaches Association (ASCA) level 5 certified coach who has been actively coaching and teaching swimming at various levels since 1986. His high school swimmers have qualified for state meets and placed in the top 10 on many occasions. At the masters level he currently coaches national champions, All-Americans, and world-record holders who have swum more than 300 top 10 U.S. Masters Swimming (USMS) swims and achieved more than 30 world records in just five years.

Throughout a career that includes coaching age-groupers, senior swimmers, and triathletes, Bay has taught thousands how to swim or how to swim better. He has written numerous articles on technique and coaching in addition to being a major contributor to the revised USMS and ASCA certification curriculum. He is a frequent presenter at clinics across the United States and has presented at the prestigious ASCA World Clinic for several years.

Coach Bay is the chair of the USMS Coaches Committee and head coach of YCF Masters, and he also coaches high school level swimming.

You'll find other outstanding swimming resources at

www.HumanKinetics.com/swimming

In the U.S. call 1-800-747-4457

Australia 08 8372 0999 • Canada 1-800-465-7301
Europe +44 (0) 113 255 5665 • New Zealand 0800 222 062

 HUMAN KINETICS
The Premier Publisher for Sports & Fitness
P.O. Box 5076 • Champaign, IL 61825-5076 USA

Steps to Success Sports Series

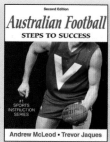

The *Steps to Success Sports Series* is the most extensively researched and carefully developed set of books ever published for teaching and learning sports skills.

Each of the books offers a complete progression of skills, concepts, and strategies that are carefully sequenced to optimize learning for students, teaching for sport-specific instructors, and instructional program design techniques for future teachers.

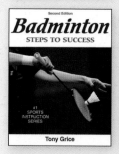
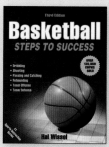
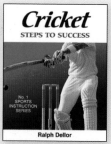

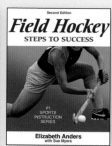

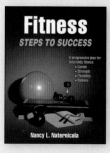

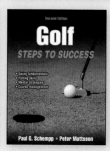
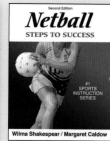
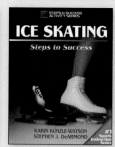
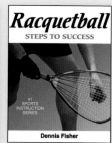

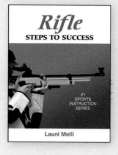
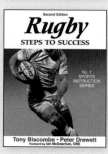
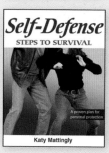
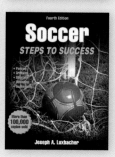
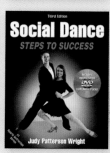
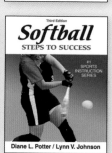

To place your order, U.S. customers call
TOLL FREE **1-800-747-4457**

In Canada call 1-800-465-7301

In Australia call 08 8372 0999

In Europe call +44 (0) 113 255 5665

In New Zealand call 0800 222 062

or visit **www.HumanKinetics.com/StepsToSuccess**

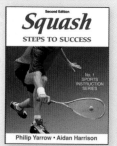
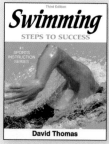
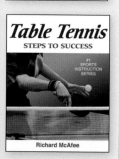

HUMAN KINETICS
The Premier Publisher for Sports & Fitness
P.O. Box 5076, Champaign, IL 61825-5076

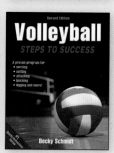